BELLA LUCIA

LUCIA'S STORY:

My Imperfect Beauty

*A Memoir written in Devotion
to and Respect for Facial Difference*

Disclaimer: most of the names of actual individuals, living and deceased, listed in this book, have been altered to protect their privacy. Discussion has been re-created from memory and various interpretations. An effort was made to uphold the vital truth of what happened and what was spoken throughout this memoir.

Beauty is not in the face; beauty is a light in the heart.

Kahlil Gibran

To be beautiful means to be yourself. You don't need to be accepted by others.

You need to accept yourself.

Thich Nhat Hanh

DEDICATION

My story is dedicated to my best friend and amazing husband, Ricky. It is written in memory of my dear mother, Marie, who, given her personal issues and many challenges as a single parent, nonetheless endeavored sincerely to create a decent home environment for me.

ACKNOWLEDGEMENTS

Along my path I have met people from various backgrounds who helped me and whom I want to thank: my family-practice physician, Ben S., M.D., who brought me into the world; professional nurses; maxillofacial surgeons, such as Dr. George S; oral surgeons and plastic surgeons such as Dr. William G. and Dr. John H.; nurses; general dentists; dental assistants; dental hygienists; prosthodontists such as Dr. Hussein Z., Dr. Craig W.; periodontists; endodontists; speech therapists such as Ali B.; social workers; counselors; friends; coworkers; and individuals with the same concerns as mine. I have had so many providers over the years that I don't remember all of their names.

In addition, I am grateful to my dearest friend, Lynn. She has been an amazing ally and support for more than thirty-six years.

The love, generosity, support, and professionalism of these people have strengthened my resolve to continue moving on in a sometimes-unfriendly world—particularly given my appearance. They believed in me, which was invaluable. Their goodness provided for me and continues to do so. They remain in my heart as strong and positive memories that assisted me in overcoming the ridicule, bullying, and rejection I sometimes faced.

I also want to express gratitude to my former writing teacher, critic, author, and editor Ivy. Her guidance, warmth, and expertise have been invaluable.

Contents

INTRODUCTION

I have been on a lifelong journey of self-discovery that for many years saw me growing each and every day. I am a woman with facial difference and have a story to share that I anticipate will make a difference to others.

This memoir reveals the experiences that have helped me to become a vibrant woman, to write my story—my poetry—to care for others professionally, and to continue to nurture myself physically, emotionally, and spiritually. I continue to care for and love myself each day, determined to remember that I am enough. This story is intended to be one of triumph, success, and inspiration. I appreciate my gift as a healer of others. This gift endures. Love and acknowledgement, honor and respect, are important gifts I provide to the world. My deserving these, too, is no different than it is for anyone else.

I feel confident I am in for additional new adventures that will give me delight! Still, I also weep in grief for what never was for me, even while I enjoy the new me that is slowly and consistently emerging. I strive to rid myself of the dishonor that was placed on me, beginning at the moment of my birth.

Releasing the fear and the shame are my goals, my reach for a more satisfying life. I am going in directions that I never before thought possible. As Emily Dickinson wrote, "I dwell in possibility." I must remember that I am a gift to the universe. I have been brought here to help myself and others remember that we all dwell in possibility and we are all connected.

With love and compassion, I celebrate who we are as human beings, that we provide encouragement for one another in all times, places, and situations. I am the butterfly emerging from the chrysalis, bursting with color. Stretching my wings and reaching many directions, I am formulating myself for takeoff into another chapter of life and discovery. My excitement is high. Writing my thoughts and expressing them brings me both tears and joy. I emerge from this to new opportunities, a vibrant world full of wonderful sounds, rainbows, and smiles, where I can express my true self without fear or judgment.

I wish for my story to touch the lives of others with facial difference as they proceed on their life journeys, to their families and friends, to their communities, and to the world. As Saint Francis of Assisi wrote during the twelfth century, "Every life needs a purpose to which it can give the energies of its mind and the enthusiasm of its heart." My purpose is a view of embracing facial difference and a life filled with love.

I found this poem in 1983 and have always had it with me. It touched me profoundly, and was the impetus for writing my memoir.

"Imperfect Beauty"
by Frank H. Keith

The rift in the chest of a mountain

The twist in the trunk of a tree.

The water-cut cave in the hollow.

The rough, rocky rim of the sea.

Each one has a scar of distortion,

Yet each has this sermon to sing.

The presence of what would deface me,

Has made me a beautiful thing.

CHAPTER 1:
A SHOCKING BIRTH

Life for me began on April 15, 1951. My birth took place in a small town in southwestern Pennsylvania, Washington. Lucia was my given name, after my paternal grandmother. My middle name is Anna after my maternal grandmother. This tradition is part of my culture, and I am thankful for it. My parents were Marie and Anthony. The constellation Aries was high in the sky that day. New life was emerging, with April showers providing new vegetation and fresh scents. But my birth was an event that caused shock and disbelief.

I was born with a severe bilateral cleft lip and palate. This congenital birth defect is caused by a failure in the formation of the soft and hard palate. The upper lip has not joined properly, is wide open and distorted, and the nose is twisted due to a lack of supporting bone and cartilage. The absent front bone, called the premaxilla, is where our front teeth are positioned. The roof of my mouth, including both soft and hard palates, was missing and there was a large opening there instead. My family's general-practice physician, Dr. Ben S., told me years later that the hole in the roof of my mouth was very deep. The floor of my nasal cavity was very obvious and easy to view.

The anatomic challenges of cleft palate include feeding and nutritional difficulties, recurrent ear infections, hearing loss, abnormal speech development, breathing and sinus problems, and facial-growth distortion. The disabled communication between the oral and nasal cavities weakens the normal sucking and swallowing ability of cleft infants. Food particles and liquids may flow back into the nasal passageway.

Second-hand information from my father's family says my appearance caused shame, fear, guilt, and anger. I have always felt shame, since the beginning of my life, that I was not conceived in love. No newborn photos were taken in the nursery at the hospital, and our parish priest baptized me in the nursery due to my projected frail condition. And yet, I began to thrive.

There was no discussion of shame, embarrassment, and guilt with my mother until years later. Finally, though, I found the courage to approach her to talk about it. When she told me that she felt responsible for my birth defect and what I had endured, I felt peace and compassion in my heart. I accepted our dilemma. It has made me a stronger and more determined individual with the ability to continue moving on with my life. I learned nothing from my father throughout our years of relationship regarding these concerns. He always told me that he loved me.

My parents took me to our parish church for a formal baptism when I was nearly a year old. I wore a long, lacy white gown with red Mary Jane shoes. I have a wonderful picture from that day of my godmother, Yolanda, holding me, which I cherish.

My mother did not find out she was pregnant with me until she was in the beginning of the second trimester or fourth month of gestation. At that time, there were no prenatal studies done such as ultrasounds, blood testing, genetic testing, or analysis of amniotic fluids.

The cause of my birth defect was not known or understood at the time. There were no known ancestors who had the same defect. It remains a mystery. As far as my immediate family knew, there was no history of cleft lip and cleft palate in our family tree. Currently, cleft lip and palate are presumed to be caused by a combination of genes and other physical factors. It might have been the environment my mother came in contact with, what she ate, drank, or took as medication during her pregnancy.

According to "Facts about Cleft Lip and Cleft Palate" from the Center for Disease Control and Prevention (CDC), research has identified some factors that increase the chance of having a baby with an orofacial (mouth, jaw, and face) cleft:

- Smoking–Women who smoke during pregnancy are more likely to have a baby with an orofacial cleft than women who do not smoke.

- Diabetes–Women with diabetes, diagnosed before pregnancy, have an increased risk of having a child with a cleft lip with or without cleft palate, compared to women who do not have diabetes.

- Use of certain medications–Women who took certain medicines, such as those to treat epilepsy—topiramate or valproic acid—during the first trimester (the first three months) of pregnancy, have an increased risk of having a baby with cleft lip with or without cleft palate, compared to women who didn't take these medications (CDC 2019, 2).

I am not sure if my mother smoked during her pregnancy; I do know she was very overweight. My suspicion is that she had gestational diabetes. I have no knowledge of her taking a medication that could have contributed to my birth defect. However, she was diagnosed with type-two diabetes when I was around age ten. The diabetes was discovered at the time of her gallbladder surgery. She took an oral anti-diabetic medication for a while. Plus, diabetes ran in my mother's family.

My mother did not reveal her health care or treatment history to me. I will never know the details, though I do have a copy of her death certificate. All of my immediate family is deceased except for one aunt who does not communicate with me. I will never know the exact cause of my birth defect. I do know the effect. It made me into what I am today: a resilient woman with imperfect beauty.

CHAPTER 2:
OCCURRENCE, REPAIR, AND MEANING BEHIND CLEFT LIP AND PALATE

Orofacial clefting occurs approximately one in seven hundred live births (cleft lip and or palate; together or alone). The prevalence varies worldwide (Drabkin 2018, 2).

The history of cleft lip reveals a fascinating phenomenon. Here is a brief synopsis from the *Indian Journal of Plastic Surgery*. The earliest acknowledged mention of cleft lip is found in texts associated with religion, superstition, invention, and even fraud in the ancient literature of Mediterranean civilizations. While Greeks ignored the existence of such birth defects, Spartans and Romans left records showing they killed these children. They were suspected of fostering evil and supernatural spirits. In Sparta, the unfortunate newborns were abandoned on Mount Tagete. In Rome, they were drowned in the Tiber River or thrown off the Tarpeian Rock. In circa 375 BCE, the philosopher Plato described this practice in one of his dialogues in the *Republic*, as a means of removing evil omens and preserving the soundness of the race.

The first documented cleft lip surgery took place in China in 390 BCE on an eighteen-year-old would-be soldier, Wey Young-Chi. Following his surgery, Wey Young-Chi was recruited into the imperial army where he quickly impressed General Lin-Yu by helping to suppress a revolt. In due course, Wey himself advanced to the rank of general and later became governor of the Province of Yee. He eventually became Governor General of the six provinces. Throughout his life, he acknowledged that he would never have accomplished so much if his cleft lip had not been repaired (Bhattacharya, Khanna, Kohli 2009, 1-4).

This story of success coincides with the initial and continuing succession of triumphant stories that emerge from the Smile Train project today. The Smile Train is a nonprofit organization and charity active in more than ninety countries that provides corrective surgery for children with cleft lips and cleft palates (Smile Train 2019, 2).

When wiser minds triumphed, Fabricius ab Aquapendente, an Italian surgeon (1537–1619) became the first to suggest the embryological basis of these clefts. Research and knowledge of cleft lip and its surgical correction received advancement during the period between the Renaissance and the nineteenth century.

Pierre Franco, a pupil of Ambroise Paré, a French surgeon (known as one of the most notable surgeons of the European renaissance) became known as the father of cleft-lip surgery. He never received formal medical education, but wrote two surgical texts based on his many years of experience: *Petit Traité* and *Traité des Hernies*. The latter was published in 1561 and in it Doctor Franco discusses the cleft lip in ample detail, devoting two chapters to the subject. He was the first to state the congenital nature of the malformation clearly and to refer to the unilateral harelip as the "lièvre fendu de nativité" (cleft lip present from birth). He provided a meticulous classification of various types of clefts, calling the bilateral harelip the "dent de lièvre" (hare's tooth) presumably because this condition was frequently accompanied by a marked protrusion of the premaxilla bone with its teeth (Bhattacharya, Khanna, Kohli 2009, 1-4).

During the nineteenth century, knowledge about surgical lip correction continued to progress, which gave parents and children with clefts optimism for a normal life. Today, multiple surgical procedures have been developed both overseas and in the United States. Strides are being made to continue advancing restorative surgeries and palliative measures to mitigate this congenital birth defect.

A *Medscape* article, "Cleft Palate Repair," addressed the development of cleft palate surgery. In summary: The first record of a palatal surgery dates back to 500 CE; prompted by inflammation of the uvula, a teardrop-shaped appendage hanging down from the soft palate. During the early nineteenth century, working to simplify procedures, surgeons and dentists in America and overseas pursued different techniques for closure such as suturing and cauterization of the edges and repair of the soft palate.

For the hard palate, surgeons worked with the bone and mucous membrane, a layer of cells that contain or secrete mucus, which is a thick fluid that protects the area from viruses and bacteria and keeps those tissues adequately moisturized in order to improve and maintain blood supply. Then, the hard palate is brought together in the middle to close the palatal cleft or split, thus preventing the surgical closure from reopening. Many advanced historical and surgical techniques have taken hold during the twentieth century.

Numerous protocols for the management of cleft lip and palate have been developed by various physicians over the years. Today, mainstream cleft repair calls for closure of the lip at an early age (from six weeks to six months) followed by closure of the palate secondarily, approximately six months later. This procedure has little negative impact on facial development.

Discussion has centered on the role and timing of pre-surgical appliances or dental prostheses such as I wore for many years. The hard palate, the root of a tooth, and the premaxilla bone that holds the front teeth can all be molded to accommodate the individual, sharing conclusive goals of facilitating surgical repair and providing an improved long-term outcome in both facial form and palatal function. These historic advances in the treatment of the cleft palate inspired progress toward today's timing for needed techniques to restore function (Patel et al, 2018, 1-3).

There is more history about the occurrence of cleft lip and palate. During the seventeenth century in colonial Salem, Massachusetts, there was much hysteria and fallacy surrounding witchcraft. If a woman was marked by the hare and her child was born with a "Hare (cleft) Lip," it was thought she had relations with Satan. This resulted in women being condemned to death (*Wide Smiles*, 1996 1-2). Sadly, this left her infant without a mother. To sum up, these tales encouraged fear of encounters, heightened by the idea that the hare might not be the harmless animal it seems. In addition, a witch in rabbit form or simply a hare alone might become a symbol of Satan.

During that time in history, women were not recognized to be equally human to a man. Injustice and distrust prevailed when many women were executed by mistake due to fabricated beliefs.

These terms and anecdotes have always been and continue to be troubling to me. I feel that they take away humanity, especially that of women who may appear to be different. Sadly, one may still hear the word "Harelip" today. I have always corrected the individual who said it and I immediately educate them about the origin of the word.

Currently, there are still injustices toward cleft lip-palate surgical restoration, outcome, and recovery in developing countries, which are chiefly influenced by superstitious sociocultural beliefs that often determine the need for consultation and medical treatment. Harmful and perceptual discriminations are relatively high, especially among the rural population of developing countries such as Africa, India, and China.

These prejudices affect the parental attachment with the child, leading to social discrimination, ridicule, stigmatization, poor psychological growth, and possible abandonment of the child, thus increasing the chance of infanticide. There is also an opposing belief that the cleft child is considered by some communities to be a gift from God with special powers, another reason for the child not to receive restorative treatment (Shirol, 2018, 2-3).

9

The need for early education and support of these families is paramount, and is being provided by amazing organizations such as Smile Train, Operation Smile, and the March of Dimes.

CHAPTER 3:
GAINING AND LOSING A SISTER

Shortly after my birth, I was taken to a large metropolitan teaching hospital in Pittsburgh, about forty-five minutes away from my hometown for evaluation and surgery. I remained in the hospital for about three months. This time is very important for infant bonding, which I missed out on receiving. So did my parents, with regard to feeding and my appearance prior to my upper lip surgical closure.

I don't know what took place, as that time of my life was not discussed. Throughout my childhood, parental attachment was inconsistent for me. I had many baby sitters, was a patient in the hospital, and adapted to being alone, entertaining myself and having an empty feeling in my home at a young age. I never witnessed my parents having any positive connection. I imagine my mother was anxious and depressed about having to care for a newborn with my birth defect, in addition to the routine care of an infant.

As stated by Robert Winston and Rebecca Chicot "Without a good initial bond, children are less likely to grow up to become happy, independent, and resilient adults." Love is the most valuable, plus a parent's time and support (2016, 12-14).

Fortunately, I had loving family members in addition to my parents who cared for me, such as my maternal grandmother, aunt, and my mother's dear friends who provided support. I do remember having a fear of abandonment. Two examples are: one day when I was seven years old, my mother and I went shopping at a five and dime store during the holidays. We became separated while I was searching for a gift. When I didn't see her, I began to panic, my heart pounding, as I hurried around the store in tears searching for her. I was so glad when I found her and she reassured me not to worry.

Another night, when I was nine, I was awoken by my mother's car engine starting at two in the morning. I jumped out of bed and ran down the steps to the dining room window, crying and yelling to my mother. I felt like she was leaving me. She assured me that she was going to pick up her boyfriend, Len, from work. She told me to get into the car while dressed in my pajamas. After we picked him up, we went to a doughnut shop and I had hot chocolate, feeling much better, calm and secure, while I savored my treats.

I also yearned for tenderness. I remember intuitively hugging our house cleaner one spring. She was a kind and friendly lady I had never met before but I felt comfortable giving her a hug. I sensed it was the right thing to do.

In the hospital, my upper lip was surgically closed. My soft and hard palates were never closed due to insufficient tissue, bone, and muscle. As far as I know, there were no complications and I tolerated the surgery well. Initially, I was fed with a medicine dropper, as specialized baby bottles and nipples were not yet developed. My ability to suck was deficient. Once they took me home, my parents did their best to care for me. Unfortunately, my mother was told by a group of elderly women at her Italian lodge that there was something wrong with her to have a baby that looked like me.

Fourteen months after my birth I gained a sister, Annmarie. She was also born with bilateral cleft lip and palate. In addition, she was born breech, feet first. Instruments were used for her delivery that resulted in cerebral palsy. My mother was devastated. Our family physician, Doctor Ben S., had told my parents after my birth that cleft lip and palate would not reoccur in the same family. Sadly, he was wrong. This second cleft child made our situation unique.

Annmarie was a frail child who eventually walked with special forearm crutches. I have a few memories of this blond, blue-eyed petite girl, even though our time of sisterhood was very short. Sharing time in the large bathtub off of our kitchen one day, she told me, "I have to pee." I yelled out to my mother and she told her to just pee in the bath water. The tub was drained and we were wrapped to dry in soft, fluffy towels.

Every day we woke up together in our cribs. My mother gently picked us up, placing one of us on her hip and the other on the opposite hip. One of my favorite breakfasts my mother prepared for us were the large shredded-wheat biscuits with warm milk poured over them. I enjoyed the taste and found them to be comforting as we sat at the kitchen table. I broke them up with my spoon when softened by the warm milk, savoring the flavor. To this day, shredded wheat is one of my favorite breakfast foods. I now eat the bite-size ones that were not available when I was a young child. I continue to appreciate this comfort food, thinking about the great taste from breakfast time with my mother.

We sat at our cozy kitchen table talking about the grocery shopping list and my mother always kept the kitchen neat and tidy. I can close my eyes and see her wearing an apron over her flowing dress, smiling as she swept the floor. The screen door of the kitchen was open as a gentle breeze came in.

Many times, Annmarie and I were dressed in the same colorful outfits. The last one I remember was a white gabardine dress with red polka dots, ruffles at the bodice, and a red ribbon belt tied in the back with a bow. We also shared a small swimming pool in the backyard on hot, humid summer days. My father always made sure we were taken care of when my mother was out of the home: naps, meals, and other physical needs.

During the winter of 1956, we both came down with the mumps. Annmarie then developed breathing problems just prior to having more restorative surgery. Her death certificate, which I found in 2019 on Ancestry.com, reported respiratory stasis and tracheobronchitis. Her lungs stopped functioning from an inflammatory affliction of her breathing passages. She died in March. She was three years old and I was four. Many years later I asked my mother what caused Annmarie's death. She told me that someone left the window open in her hospital room and she accepted that, which troubled me, increasing my anger and sadness.

I remember my mother coming to me and asking me to give my colorful, beaded rosary bracelet to Annmarie. She was going away and would never return. She was very sad and solemn. Later, I learned that the bracelet was placed on her wrist in the casket. At her funeral, a Roman Catholic Angel Mass service took place. Her pallbearers were all little girls.

Final goodbyes were not possible at the cemetery. My mother was disappointed on the day of the funeral because it was so bitter cold and icy, the ground rock hard, so Annmarie's burial plot could not be excavated. Fortunately, the next day the ice melted and the sun was shining. I was not able to attend her funeral or interment. I was home with my grandmother, Anna, recovering from the mumps. My mother's piercing cries and sorrowful weeping were heard throughout the house during the memorial luncheon. Annmarie's passing was very painful for my parents.

In 2010, I contacted Janice, my cousin on my father's side of the family, while working on my family tree. At the time, I was completing post-graduate work. I had not seen or spoken to her for about fifty years. She was generous with sharing Annmarie's death notice, which I had not seen. It was a short clipping from the local newspaper. I cherish the clipping to this day.

Janice confided to me that both my and my sister's birth defects brought shame to the family. She did much research before becoming pregnant so she would not have a child with the same birth defect. She stated that her genetic counselor told her that my mother had to have been taking a medication that caused our birth defects. In addition, she provided details regarding my father's family tree, my paternal grandmother's maiden name, and other family specifics. I was grateful to receive that information. We continue to stay in touch regarding our ancestry.

I wrote this poem to honor Annmarie's memory:

"Sisterhood: For Dear Annmarie"

Sisterhood is great.

I wish I had a sibling.

For sharing smiles.

For recalling memories.

Tub baths, bubbles, laughter,

Tears and scraped knees.

Finding acceptance

During those teenage years

Yearning for true love,

Growing in courage,

Two women with integrity.

Becoming ourselves.

Enjoying aging,

Together as family,

Our own special moments.

This will never be.

My sister has long been gone.

Still, I feel her spirit.

Not much was said about Annmarie after her passing, unless someone asked questions. Family secrets were always kept. My parents continued to work opposite shifts. My mother was the chief switchboard operator at the local hospital and worked the day shift. My father was a laborer at the local glass factory and worked the evening shift. My parents' marriage had been arranged the old Italian way. They were not spiritually related. They slept in separate rooms. I never felt there was love between them.

Looking at the positive side, they made a home for me. I am sure this was not easy for them and they did their best to care for me as well as they could during their strained relationship, until their separation.

CHAPTER 4:
SWEET MEMORIES
OF MY FATHER

I have many fond memories of my father from those first six years of my life. He was a tender, nurturing man with a giving heart. My big thrill was when he came home from the glass factory, bringing me a Hershey's York Peppermint Patty. At age five, that was the best treat! It felt so big in my little hand. Today, York Peppermint Patties continue to be one of my favorite treats. I think of my dad each time I bite into one. This poem attests to that.

"Sweet Memories"

With every bite

I have sweet memories.

Each and every time

Days gone by return

With that York Peppermint Patty

Taste buds come alive

Dad arrived home

At night from the glass factory

Hugs and a surprise

My eyes were wide

With excitement I reached

For the round candy bar

Being five years old

I would look forward to this gift

Perfect in my hand

Mint and chocolate

My special treat

Our time together

Each taste is pure bliss

From such a simple pleasure

From my dear father

My father is gone.

And this candy is found everywhere!

I am so happy

Today I continue

To love York Peppermint Patty

With sweet memories

With each bite I take,

I know that he is with me,

Smiling upon me.

Thank you, Daddy

Other memories of my father include him grooming my hair, taking me to kindergarten on the bus, holding my hand, and pulling my sled up the snow-covered road, with me sitting on it, in order to visit my paternal grandparents during the Christmas holidays. He put up a swing set in the back yard; that was also special. I learned to pump the swing, with his help, and swing high. Swinging on swings continues to be one of my favorite activities when I am near a playground. I feel my dad close by. And, I proudly learned how to tie my shoe with his praise.

An incident I will never forget occurred when I was five and my father rescued me from a heartless babysitter. One evening while he was working and my mother was out, the sitter was giving me a bath. I kept telling her that the water was too hot. I felt like I was getting burned. The skin on my legs and belly had numerous pink blotches. She refused to cool the water. I started to cry. Much to my amazement, my father rushed into the bathroom, wrapped me in a towel, and carried me to a nearby bed. He then promptly asked the sitter to leave. I did not sustain any injury. What a rescue! I felt safe and loved. The sitter was never asked into our home again.

Another time, during the summer when I was around six, my father came from our hometown by bus to visit me in the hospital. The hospital staff informed us that I would be discharged that day. All I had was my underwear and fuzzy, trimmed slippers. So, the nurses gave me a pink and blue flowered dress with a wide, white collar and puffy short sleeves to wear home. I felt happy and cared for, loving my new dress. We had a pleasant trip home on the bus. I wasn't concerned about my appearance; I was just happy being with my father. Holding his hand while crossing the street brought me a safe and tranquil feeling.

My father was a strong, gentle man with kind blue eyes, off-black hair, and a medium build. He took care of us and our home. He made sure the front and back lawns were groomed and maintained. We had small, colorful statues of ducks and rabbits in our yard. I always felt protected when he was present. He had an elementary school education and was unable to read and write fluently. I imagine this is the reason he did not have a driver's license. And even though he didn't drive a car, he always had a job.

My warmest memories of our relationship come from those first six years.

CHAPTER 5:
A NEW PROSTHETIC DEVICE
AND IMPROVED SPEECH

I also have fond memories of my bedroom. There were circus animals on my curtains, bears and elephants standing on their hind legs leaning on red and blue drums. The ceiling had stars that glowed in the dark. I remember having my Tiny Tears doll lying at my side, she was covered by a blue satiny layette with white lace trim and a pink ribbon. Sometimes I felt lonely and scared without Annmarie. Lying in my bed at night and clutching my doll in fear, I stared across the room. A crucifix hung on the opposite wall. I was then able to fall asleep.

During this time, I had difficulty speaking clearly. Eating and drinking were also a challenge due to my missing hard and soft palates. The bone where my upper teeth should be was incomplete, and a few teeth came in crooked. The teeth and their roots were surgically removed by putting me to sleep with general anesthesia and pulling them out, which was a common practice during that time period. I can remember running my tongue along the suture line with the hanging threads until they came out.

Orange juice was my favorite drink during my hospital surgery stays, but I quickly had my fill of Jell-O, soup, and hot cereal. The consistency and taste of Jell-O did not set well with me, and I have not eaten it for years, but I still like hot oatmeal, hot wheat cereal, and soup during the cold months.

Many times, moist food and fluids went up into my nose. I could not use a straw due to my inability to suck and due to air leaks. Ice cream was a treat; however, I was unable to lick it from a cone. I couldn't keep up with the melting ice cream dripping down the sides of the cone onto my hand. I retreated to eating my ice cream in a cup with a spoon, which I still continue to do and have for many years.

Relief to restore my open soft and hard cleft palates arrived when I was about six. I was fitted for my first prosthesis, also called an obturator or an appliance. These terms can be used interchangeably.

It was an extensive process. First, grooved metal rings were plastered on my two upper teeth on each side. Then impressions were taken using a metal tray that fit my mouth and upper teeth. Trying to keep the dental plaster from going into my nose and down my throat was difficult. Sometimes, I vomited. When the prosthesis was complete, I had three false front teeth attached to the front of the obturator as restoration for my own missing teeth. Wires on the side were fitted over the rings on my upper side teeth.

On the back of the obturator was a plastic, opaque bulb that measured one centimeter high and two centimeters wide. It improved my eating skills and helped me to speak, suck, and avoid the frequent backflow of food and fluids. The obturator had the appearance of a lobster without claws as it attached to the metal rings. It covered the areas of my absent soft and hard palates. It was removable, like false teeth, for daily cleaning. I tried to remember to do this when I brushed my teeth, but it was not always an easy feat to be completed by a child. Sometimes I skipped a day or two and food particles collected underneath the obturator, leading to bad breath. What a mess! As I grew into my teens, I took the obturator out at night and soaked it in a dental cup. I was lucky not to have cavities, but my gums were affected with inflammation and receded, leading to minor surgery to remove the affected gum tissue.

I received a new prosthetic appliance every three years as I grew until I had my soft and hard palates surgically closed at age thirty-seven. It was tough when I had a new prosthesis made; the old one was taken and used to make the new one during my years in grade school and high school. Without my obturator, while waiting for my new one, it was embarrassing to eat, drink, and speak in public. This contributed to low self-esteem and seclusion. Being around my peers was very uncomfortable during this time. I spoke little for fear of ridicule.

Dental hygiene continued to be an important task because of the possibility of food fragments getting stuck underneath my prosthesis. I worked hard at this as I matured into adulthood, receiving guidance from my dentists, periodontists, and dental hygienists.

I began speech therapy at age five, which continued until I was ten. The weekly sessions included repetitive oral exercises, listening to my teacher, and listening to myself speak on a tape recorder. Sometimes I was asked to speak into a milk carton cut on the side. My speech therapist praised my ability to catch on quickly. She was very encouraging, creating milestones for success. This accomplishment helped to ease my shyness and raise my self-confidence.

CHAPTER 6:
MY PARENTS' DIVORCE
AND WHAT FOLLOWED

When I was between the ages of four and six, while we all still lived together following Annmarie's death, my parents argued much of the time. I remember hearing them shouting in their bedroom while I stood at the top of the stairs of our home. There was little connection between them. My mother pretty much did activities with her friends or her family members. Even then, I do not recall many family gatherings, except on our birthdays. These gatherings were usually with my maternal aunts, uncles, and cousins, and my mother's friends from her work. I felt that my parent's families were separated. As an example, I used to walk alone to and from church every Sunday because my mother declined to go with me. One

Sunday I saw my paternal uncle Joe and his wife, my aunt Marcella. I began to greet them. They looked away and walked past me as if I were not there. I felt so sad and snubbed.

Growing up in a small town was awful for me. The heartache and anxiety of wanting to be accepted by family and friends brought on a desire to isolate myself, even more so given my fear of rejection by anyone I met and feel even more humiliation. Receiving little support, the addition of family issues did not help. Our home was sad after the loss of Annmarie. There were times when I wondered why my life was not taken instead of hers. I missed her and often felt so blue and alone. This contributed to me feeling timid, afraid to ask for what I wanted, because I dreaded rejection.

These feelings of shame, fear of rejection, and sadness have decreased over the years. However, they do haunt me at times, when triggers from the past reopen old traumas. When painful memories do resurface, I visualize them in my mind, such as how I never felt at home in my childhood home. Then I remember how far I have come on my journey and how much I have accomplished on my own. This led to my ambition to leave as soon as I was able to live and work independently.

My mother purchased a car and gained confidence driving so she was able to transport us thirty-five miles into Pittsburgh in order for me to continue my needed care at the cleft-palate and cranio-facial clinic. We no longer had to take public transportation. I was glad not to have to take two buses and a streetcar. The diesel fumes from the buses caused me to have nausea and vomiting. My mother always had a paper bag available, just in case I needed it.

Following the completion of kindergarten in the spring of 1957, I eagerly entered first grade that autumn. One August evening my mother came to me and said that we were moving. All of our belongings were packed into her car. We were leaving our furniture behind. I remember looking through tears out the back window, staring toward the driveway, already missing my dad and my swing set. Even now, I can envision that time and feel the hurt.

My mother filed for divorce, based on my father's sexual preferences. He wanted to be with men, which I didn't know until I was around twenty. My mother did maintain a relationship with my father's younger sister over the years, my aunt Tess. One Sunday we were visiting my aunt while my father was there. He needed transportation to his home and my mother gave him a ride. I felt confused as we rode together in the car. Nothing else was said. I was surprised that my mother would do this for him. In my young mind, a divorce meant no more contact with your former spouse. When we got to my father's destination, he thanked my mother when he got out of the car. This was a generous gesture on my mother's part.

My mother did take me to see my paternal grandfather the day I made my first Holy Communion, which I enjoyed. During my school days, I saw my father sometimes for dinner and shopping, mainly for my birthday and Christmas.

I did not see my father again until my high school graduation party in 1969, and then not again until 1972, when I graduated from nursing school. He just showed up, unexpectedly. I was glad to see my father at these events. He was warm and loving toward me, as usual. At my nursing graduation party, he told me he was proud of me. This made me feel special and valued.

Unfortunately, I did not have a relationship with my paternal grandmother, Lucia. She preferred not to learn to speak English, and was only comfortable talking Italian, which I knew very little of. Our immediate family was encouraged to speak English since we were Americans. I now see this as an unfortunate barrier for a connection. I only saw her a few times after my parents divorced, and did not get to see her before she died when I was eight years old. My mother did not take me to any of my grandmother Lucia's funeral events. My memories of my paternal grandparent's home are of rooms pleasantly smelling of fresh garlic when I walked in, and there was always warm homemade Italian bread.

After we moved from my first home, we moved into a first-floor apartment with my mother's boyfriend, Len. I had my own bedroom. I had to finish first grade at another public school. I made new friends and excelled in drawing and painting. Shortly after this, we moved to a third-floor apartment in the same building. My mother initiated my attending classes at a school of dance just down the street. I became proficient in tap and ballet. I made my debut at the yearly review show, where I tapped to the song, *Five Foot Two, Eyes of Blue*. My outfit was hot pink and black, with a small black tutu trimmed with pink satin ribbon. Len painted my black tap shoes silver. My black banana curls bounced as I tapped. My photo was taken and transferred onto a wooden block that I was supposed to receive, but my mother failed to return to pick it up. It was also disappointing that she and other family members and friends never came to any of my weekly classes after school, to support me as I progressed.

One summer afternoon when I was six my mother left me alone with some neighborhood children. My friend Sandy and I hid under the large porch on the front of our apartment house and ate coconut bonbons out of the box. When my mother returned home, she scolded me for not being with the adult family of my friend next door and told me never to tell my father what happened. I was not scolded for sitting in the dirt. I imagine she feared losing custody of me because she had left me with no adult supervision. I just played with my friend and was left alone. There were adults in the house next door where Sandy lived. No one came by to check on us and I never did tell my father about it.

I attended a third school, Saint Hilary Catholic Grade School, where I celebrated my first Holy Communion. My mother's friend Rose and her family lived nearby. They took me in on the weekends so that my mother and Len could go dancing on Saturday nights. I became friends with Rose's daughter, Patsy. She always had frilly petticoats and anything else she wanted.

A frightening incident took place when I was in the third grade. One snowy, dark, and frigid Sunday evening when Mom was supposed to pick me up at Rose's home and take me home, she called, requesting that I take the bus because the weather was too bad for her to drive over. On an icy street, I made my way to the bus stop about a block away from Rose's house. I waited for the bus. As it came by, I walked across the ice and fell. As I struggled to crawl on the ice and get up, I fell again. By this time, the bus drove past me around the corner. I lay on the ice crying, feeling so cold. I was shivering. There were no cars or people on the street. Wet and in tears, I struggled to crawl on the ice, sliding to get back on my feet until I reached snow-covered ground. I stood up, deeply afraid of being scolded for missing the bus.

I made my way back to Rose's home and called my mother to inform her. From what I remember, she was okay with it. I was told to stay the night there. I was glad to be back in a warm house and feel welcomed. I changed into dry clothing and enjoyed some hot cocoa. It felt good to know I could stay overnight and miss school the next morning.

When I became ten, Rose told me that she didn't want me to be her daughter's friend anymore, that she had other friends. This rejection caused me bewilderment and it really hurt my feelings. I felt like I didn't have cute things like Patsy and that I was not as pretty because of my facial difference. Nothing more was ever said by Rose, my mother, or Patsy. After that, I made no effort to connect with Patsy until we were adults and had each suffered family losses. But we never reconnected as friends.

That summer in 1959 we had a one-bedroom apartment on the second floor above a printing press. I didn't have my own bedroom, so I slept in the living room. The next year we moved again, this time to the projects. Again, I didn't have my own bedroom. Each time, Mom's boyfriend, Len, was with us. In part because my mother never picked up my picture on the block and because I missed dance school due to my school being further away from home, I was angry and withdrew from people. Luckily, I was introduced to the Brownie Scouts. I enjoyed the group activity and selling Girl Scout cookies. My Girl Scout leader was very supportive, warm, and welcoming. I made friends with the other girls. No bullying took place.

My mother made the effort so that I could be involved in these various activities. Still, I had shallow feelings about family and no spiritual connection. Mostly, tenderness was missing from my childhood. Hugs and kisses did not occur often. I got scolded for getting sick, or having a cold, chapped lips, or a runny nose. For many years when I got sick, I became scared, fearful about telling my mother and anticipating being reprimanded for something over which I had no control.

I was taught not to talk, feel, or even think about family matters. We never talked about my birth defect. Over the years, I felt I was treated as if I didn't have any brains. This lack of sincerity, validation, and acceptance hurt. There was too much negativity and a paucity of communication, which lead me to develop feelings of anger and pain.

Unfortunately, as I grew older my fear of my mother increased. I felt I was a problem for her, always in the way. Even into adulthood, I felt less than others when my mother questioned my personal decisions or my conversations with others. This contributed to my struggle with self-acceptance and the desire for freedom and peace within myself. This situation reinforced my goal to be around supportive people with a loving point of view.

My favorite place to stay was with my widowed grandmother, Anna. I felt safe and welcomed in her home. Grandma was short and stout with a gentle demeanor, bright brown eyes, and a beautiful smile. She always wore an apron over her dress. She told me I had the memory of an elephant when I recited what I had read or heard at school. We made homemade Italian bread with butter for breakfast and I went into the cellar, as we called it, with her to put coal in the furnace on cold winter days. I played with her cat, Tom, and took short walks to the neighborhood store down the hill. Her company raised my spirits.

In addition, when I played in the middle of the road in dirt and gravel, my cousin Michael who lived down the street was very protective of me when other children came by making fun of my appearance. He said, "Leave her alone," which felt so kind and loving. Michael made it comfortable for me to play outside without fear of bullying. I really appreciated that; it is a fond and affirmative memory. Unfortunately, I did not maintain contact with Michael over the years, but I will never forget his kindness and his spirit.

Clearly, I learned a great deal about life at an early age. I had experienced the death of my only sibling, the loss of our home, the room I loved, my parents' divorce, separation from my father, and, above all, a congenital birth defect that would affect the rest my life—not only because I saw it every day in the mirror, but because of the emotional, physical, social, and spiritual hurt that came my way because of it.

My yearnings to have a face without deformity, to speak fluently without fear of mockery, and to eat and drink without aspirating up into my nose and no longer need my appliance were always on my mind. The love and the peacefulness I craved, which I could have shared with my sister, were lacking. Thus, it was a double loss for me.

An optimistic experience for me was when my mother and I made many trips to Pittsburgh. I was a regular at the Cleft Palate / Craniofacial Clinic. Each year I met with the dentist, prosthodontist, maxillofacial/oral surgeon, social worker, speech therapist, and psychotherapist. It took all day to see everyone for these evaluations. A number card was pinned on my chest and checked off to keep track of each appointment. Mom and I were glad when it was all completed. We enjoyed lunch together, even if I couldn't use a straw because my obturator was taken away to make me a new one. I had to be careful not to aspirate fluids or wet food up into my nose. It became an artistic feat. Another treat from my mother was receiving a toy or clothes for my baby dolls or myself from the five and dime store about a block away from the clinic.

One incident took place during my time at the clinic that I will never forget. I had a tooth pulled by the dentist, Doctor McNally, without being told it was going to happen and without local anesthesia. I remember crying in pain, blood running down my chin, as I tightly held the dental assistant's hand. This traumatic memory stuck with me for years. I reminded this same dentist in passing about the event when I was an adult in my twenties and, luckily, receiving care from another dentist. I associated pain and trauma with that event and the insensitive dentist having no regard for my feelings, especially given I was a child with facial difference.

One day when I was six, I decided to chew bubblegum with my friend. When all of the taste went out of it, I swallowed it. Or so I thought. The bubblegum went up into one of my nostrils and became stuck there. My mother tried to get it out without success and took me to our family physician, Dr Ben, who spotted the gum high up in my nostril. He placed long forceps up my nose, which caused me to cry and squirm on the exam table. After what seemed like several minutes, the wad of bubblegum was removed. My mother and I were so relieved. To this day, I won't chew any kind of gum.

What was most difficult for me was that my mother never told me that, even though I had this birth defect, I was fine as a person. The word cleft was never mentioned. Instead, the term hare lip was used. I felt I was not as good as everyone else. It was like I was not a whole person. Some of my teachers and other adults treated me like I had little intelligence.

These experiences added to my determination to go forward with what I wanted to do in my life and not to stop. A seed was planted to extend myself and be my best self in order to make up for my birth defect. I was determined to show the world that I was very intelligent and that I had the courage to succeed, no matter how my face was perceived, acknowledging that I had an imperfect beauty that was exceptional.

CHAPTER 7:
ALCOHOL AND
PARENTAL CONFUSION

My mother worked full-time and made efforts to provide a good home life. For instance, she made sure I made it to all of my dental and surgery appointments, that I had the latest clothing even if it was a hand-me-down, visits with family and friends, short trips to amusement parks, and ate out at our favorite restaurants.

But a major component of our relationship was missing for me. My mother showed little compassion and tenderness for me. Warmth and affection were minimal. I was disciplined very strictly and felt my mother didn't trust me. This, of course, gave me angst. For example, during my high school years, I was not permitted to go out with my friends to school dances and movies on the weekends until the whole upstairs of the house was cleaned. Also, there was no driving education at my high school, but my mother still refused to teach me how to drive. She would not let me touch her car until I learned how to drive from someone else and I purchased my own car and obtain my own insurance.

On one occasion when I was twenty, sitting on the arm of a chair that my mother sat in, I attempted to hug her. She called me "a lesbian." This was baffling to me. I felt rejected and hurt. All I wanted was some affection from my mother. Maybe she felt strange about this incident because my father was homosexual. This was another mystery for me.

Her boyfriend, Len, continued to reside with us and provide some support when he was not drinking alcohol. I quickly learned that he had a problem with drinking. He and my mother argued most of the time. There was much shouting of obscenities between them. When he came home, he talked to me incessantly with his stinky breath. My mother made him angry, and then the fighting and throwing of objects began. Holidays became sad because he often came home late and intoxicated. Our beautifully decorated home, which he had helped to enhance when he was sober, stunk of alcohol. This was not easy for my mother, causing her frustration and anger. Making Christmas cookies together while playing carols on the record player helped to make the season lighter. I learned much about baking traditional biscotti and pizzelle cookies.

One evening in 1960, my mother was out and my grandmother Anna was babysitting. Len came home very drunk and became furious that my mother was not at home. My grandmother was very fearful of his behavior. She asked him to go. When leaving, he slammed his whole right arm through the glass window of our front door. Blood and glass were everywhere in the hallway. He sustained injuries that required urgent medical attention. I don't remember the details that followed, I just remember his arm required several stitches. Unfortunately, my mother's and Len's relationship continued for many years despite the volatility.

I was happy to be attending Immaculate Conception grade school. It was the fourth and last elementary school I attended. I was able to get back into dance class, following a year-long absence. I did so well with tap that my teacher let me lead the class. That year I tapped to *The Peppermint Twist*. My white costume had bright red fringe that looked like the stripes were moving when we danced. Dancing was such an accomplishment for me. I always felt beautiful as I moved my arms and legs to the rhythm.

According to my mother, my father was avoiding me. She said that she had to contact him in order for me to receive Christmas and birthday gifts. I learned, too, that he had lived in my hometown the whole time I was growing up. I didn't know this and didn't get to see him. It causes me sadness, still, when I think about the loss of our relationship for so many years. When I disobeyed my mother, she threatened to send me to my father. I became confused. My father took me shopping and to dinner a few times, but then I didn't see him for six years. Alimony and child support stopped when I turned twelve. My mother made no effort to have it reinstated. I have no idea why.

In 2009, I received another piece of information from my godmother. She said there had been a superstition that God had punished my father for his sexual preference of homosexuality, caus-ing him to have two children born with birth defects. I found this information distressing and ludicrous.

CHAPTER 8:
COPING WITH BULLYING
AND ENJOYING OTHER
LOVING RELATIONSHIPS

In the latter part of 1960, when I was nine, we finally moved into a five-room, two-story house. I was thrilled to have my own bedroom with two windows. We had no air conditioning, but it felt fine to just have a fan. I got used to the warm, sticky Pennsylvania nights.

One night around two in the morning, I was awakened to the sound of my mother yelling at her boyfriend. Len had laid down beside me in my bed. He was tipsy and ended up in the wrong bedroom. She yelled profanities at him as he moved to their bedroom. In addition, he had urinated on a bushel basket of fresh, clean laundry, which left my mother even more infuriated.

I was now in the fourth grade. I met new neighbors who became my close friends. After turning ten, I secured my first job. I walked two children to and from school each day: Iris, age nine, and her brother, Francis, who was six. Payment for my efforts included my first human anatomy book for kids. I was excited when I saw all of the colorful pictures. The images of the heart, guts, muscles, and bones fascinated me. I felt so light and airy, wanting to learn more about them! I thought about what it would be like to cut open a frog and couldn't imagine doing it.

On cold, snowy days we got a ride to school from my neighbor's father, Jack. It was so nice not to have to walk in the chilly temperatures and falling snow. This family was very warm toward me, and I felt like an honorary member. I was always welcomed into their home and even got to spend time with their extended family up the street.

I continued to take dance classes. My final tap dance review included *The Stars and Stripes Forever*. My costume was red, white, and blue. I was happy to perform this dance at the yearly recital and sad that it was my last. Dancing was such a soothing and pleasurable way for me to express myself. Now, I had to leave it. The next year, at fourteen, I went to work at my first formal job, in the dietary department at Washington Hospital.

Throughout those years, I continued to have restorative surgery on my mouth, upper lip, gums, and nose and have my obturator reconstructed so it fit my growing mouth. It wasn't easy for me. It was painful and embarrassing at times, yet it brought me hope for the future. I could feel the progress I was making. I coped by staying active with work and school and by having relationships with other women near my mother's age who became substitute mothers for me.

My mother continued to make sure I made it to appointments and surgeries. We never missed any of them. I know she wanted the best for me and for me to receive the care I needed to progress in life.

I had been a latchkey kid since I was seven. My mother usually came home from work around five o'clock. When I was ten and walking home alone from school on a snowy day, a boy came out of nowhere and threw a snowball, which directly hit my right eye. I can still see his freckled face, impish grin and strawberry-colored hair peeking out from his knit cap. He immediately ran away and I cried the remainder of my walk home as the chilly pain penetrated my eye. He had shouted something demeaning, but I don't remember what. Luckily, my vision was not impaired and there were no major injuries. Bullying was a part of my life, and it contributed to my anger.

When I saw beautiful girls and women in magazines, I took a black pencil and struck lines through their upper lips. I thought about my facial scars and wished I did not have to deal with them every day, crying in despair. This led to my dislike of beauty pageants on television, seeing them as women being chosen mainly for their beauty and less for their intelligence and talent.

Another incident of bullying came from my cousin, Sam, in Ohio while I was visiting his family. This cousin was downright cruel to me. He made fun of me. One day we were waiting in line at the soda fountain at the local drug store when he placed a large wad of bubblegum down my back, pushing my clothing against it and my skin. It was not a pleasant experience to get the gum removed. My aunt Sonja and my cousin Tricia struggled to help me release the sticky clump from my skin. My dislike for Sam was reinforced.

In addition, during fifth grade, I exchanged notes with two boys who were friendly toward me. Just as I passed a note to Ed in front of me, my teacher, Mrs. Smallman, ordered me to come to the front of the room. She scolded me, lifting the back of my dress in front of everyone. Then she paddled me on my underwear-covered buttocks. I felt sad and embarrassed. Luckily, there was no physical injury.

Too embarrassed, I did not tell my mother. I don't remember anyone at the school ever talking about it. Years later, I saw that teacher in church during Sunday service but did not say anything to her. To this day, I can still see her pale face and red, graying hair. I will never forget her name. In today's world, this teacher would have been charged with child abuse.

By contrast, my grade school friends were important to me—they were another family for me. I felt supported and loved, always welcomed in their homes. I will never forget them. My friend Stephanie, her three sisters, and her parents, treated me like another sibling. Our friendship began when we were eight and continues even today though we don't live close to one another anymore. I have so much love and respect for Stephanie and her sisters. They will live forever in my heart.

The year 1962 was rough for me because my grandmother, Anna, died from complications of diabetes. Unfortunately, she had declined medical attention. A leg amputation resulted from a cut she sustained on her heel. This was followed by a stroke that eventually led to her demise. Luckily, I was able to visit her while she was in the hospital. I continue to miss her love, support, tenderness, and care. I cherish the times I had and the memories I keep of her. I feel that she is with me every day.

Another major person in my life was my godmother, Yolanda. I called her my spiritual mother. She was always supportive of me, from birth until her passing in 2015. She attended many of my important events: my recoveries from surgery when I was hospitalized, my first Holy Communion, my Confirmation, my high school graduation, my graduation from nursing school, and my graduation when I received a master of science degree in nursing. Our relationship lasted until her passing, and my relationship with her family continues. We always had fun celebrating her favorite color, purple. I enjoyed giving her something purple every Christmas, gifts from a shawl to a paring knife. In fact, at her funeral she lay in her casket dressed in purple. Everyone in the family and all her friends wore purple to honor her. I will never forget her love and her tenderness, welcoming me into her family.

When I turned fourteen, I told my mother that I wanted to attend Immaculate Conception High School so I could be with my friends. My mother informed me that in order to afford the tuition and my school uniforms, I needed to start working. She was instrumental in my getting a job because she was a supervisor at Washington Hospital.

I worked in the Washington Hospital dietary department all through high school, from 1965 to 1969. I worked three hours each evening after school four days a week, and eight to sixteen hours on many weekends. This was a great time for me to meet interesting and warm people of all ages and from different high schools with whom I became friends. I learned so much from the multiple jobs that I held there. I learned to clean dirty dishes efficiently, prepare food in large quantities for the hospital patients, and to deliver them with care, to serve food in the cafeteria, and to try new kinds of food I had not eaten at home. My supervisors praised my work, proclaiming me a Jack of all Trades.

Looking back, I am grateful for this job during my high school years. It gave me an opportunity to expand my social skills and practice my self-acceptance. It did affect my schoolwork in that I was not encouraged about working hard in school. However, I was able to make average grades, despite my long working hours.

While on the job, when I was fifteen, I met my first boyfriend, Max. We went to a local amusement park where I received my first kiss in the Tunnel of Love, on the water ride. Our relationship was short. Years later he married, served in Vietnam, and was injured by shrapnel. He did survive. As far as I know, he had multiple injuries, resulting in much pain, and eventually he died. I will always remember Max.

My high school years were awkward, typical for adolescents, but mine was more. I felt less than others and self-conscious. I didn't feel comfortable looking at myself in the girls' bathroom mirror while my fellow classmates primped their hair and makeup. I found it to be a waste of time because I believed I wasn't pretty like the other girls. So, I walked away. I had a habit of looking down when I walked in public for many years. This dissipated over time as I began to feel better about myself.

I was never asked to go to a prom. I sensed that I wasn't in the same category as the other girls at my high school. I accepted it at the time, but it was sad for me. I felt that I lacked the style and affluence. Being the child of a single, working mother. However, I attended the frequent high school dances with my friends. Which I excelled in, loving to dance to the rock and roll hits at the time. I moved with rhythm and grace. Feeling elated on the dance floor.

As time went by, I envisioned I would be at a special event looking attractive in a black dress. This daydream came true after meeting my current husband, Ricky. In 2002, we attended a Valentine's Day dance at the school of nursing where I was teaching. I got to wear an attractive black dress. We joked that this was our prom as we danced to live music, thoroughly enjoying the evening. My vision became real!

Another incident involved a female high school classmate. Trish yelled out to me while I was crossing the street and greeting a young man whom I knew from my job. "Oh, why would he want to say hi to you? Who would want you?" This was just another bullying behavior that caused me to have melancholy and anxiety.

One difficult surgical event for me took place around this time, when surgeons tried to get my nose to be straight. It kept drawing over to the left side, resulting in my left nostril being smaller than my right one. This impaired my breathing, especially when I had a cold or sinus infection, which occurred often. At seventeen I had another rhinoplasty, or in slang, a nose job to correct my crooked nose and improve the scarring on my upper lip. The skin on my upper lip was made smoother, so it no longer had an orange-peel appearance. I gained more poise as my appearance improved, which helped me with my career growth, even though my nose was not straight. My hospital roommate, Gloria, was having a rhinoplasty for cosmetic reasons. How I wished I were like her. She was very kind and she was lovely, even before the surgery. She reported that her nose was too big and she wanted it to be smaller. I remember thinking, *I wish that was all I had to do to become normal!* There were still many milestones ahead for me.

Female adults who worked with my mother treated me as lesser and caused me to feel inferior. But there was one great friend, Marta, who was the exception. She was like another mother, accepting and supportive. Her saying was, "Your mother got something out of her marriage and that was you." We remained close friends over the years, as she and her husband, Bob, welcomed me into their new home in Arizona. They let me drive their vehicle and spend time with their black Labrador retriever, Magic. Marta died in 1999. I was so glad to be able to visit her before her passing. I have fond and loving memories of this wonderful woman who touched my life with unconditional love.

CHAPTER 9:
EMBARKING ON
HIGHER EDUCATION

I originally dreamed of being a professional dancer, becoming one of the Rockettes, kicking up my legs at Rockefeller Center in New York, or one of the June Taylor dancers on television. At age twelve, a nun at my middle school discouraged me from pursuing that route. She said it would be a rough life. So, nursing became my career path.

During the multiple times I was in the hospital for surgeries as a child and as an adolescent, I remember the tender and loving care I received from the nurses. They changed my surgical dressings, made sure I was bathed and fed, and they brought me my favorite snacks. In fact, as a child following one hospital stay, I didn't want to go home. I felt loved and supported by the nurses, doctors, and staff. I knew then that this profession was the one for me to pursue.

On a personal level, I credit Aunt Caterina for assisting me with my hair and makeup. When I visited her in Ohio during my preteen and teenage years, she took me to her stylist to assist with my hair. I felt so pampered and elegant with my new hairstyle. I got very little coaching from my mother when it came to hairstyle and appearance. She seemed too busy with her work and community life. She was the president of the ladies lodge, a division of The Sons of Italy in America. Monthly meetings were held, oriented toward my Italian heritage and public events.

During my elementary school years, my aunt Caterina was a teenager. She took me to drive-in movies, drive-in restaurants, and to the pool with her friends. I have fond memories of her, feeling loved and cared for, a sweet bond.

Once I had set my goal to be a professional nurse, I pursued the sciences, chemistry and biology, and advanced mathematics while I worked at the hospital. I successfully graduated from Immaculate Conception High School in 1969. My grades were average.

My first attempt at nursing education was to apply to the diploma school of nursing at my local hospital. The director of the school of nursing told my mother that I did not score high enough on the reading portion of the National League of Nursing entrance exam, so I would "never make it" and would have to drop out after a few months. Only "the cream of the crop" were accepted into the program. I was offended by the insensitive rejection, mostly because the information was not given to me directly—as an adult— but to my mother. I proved them wrong when I was accepted at another nursing school and went on to advance my career. Years later, following my successful completion of a bachelor of science nursing degree, I was asked to return to teach at the school that rejected me. I declined.

Applying to other schools, I was accepted into Braddock General Hospital School of Nursing in Braddock, Pennsylvania. I am thankful to the Forty and Eight Veteran's Association for the scholarship they gave me and to the Department of Vocational Rehabilitation for other financial support I received that helped me complete my nursing education. My mother was relieved to only have to pay for my health insurance.

I graduated from high school in June and entered nursing school in August of 1969. The years in nursing school were a time of deep learning and personal growth. I especially loved anatomy and physiology. And I was proud that I made it on the Dean's List.

Part of my learning included a laboratory exam naming all of the bones and human body parts on display, which made education and memorization fun. In fact, I was so fascinated by my first autopsy, that I wrote an English class essay about it when I attended Duquesne University to pursue my bachelor of science nursing degree. The essay was very descriptive of my curiosity and my experience. Seeing a once alive cadaver and learning the cause of his death. My professor, who also wrote children's books, encouraged me to continue writing. I have. Today, the function of the human body and its physiological operations are still just amazing to me. Each system has its own unique function, such as the heart, the brain, and the endocrine system, to name just a few.

I also made some dear friends while at nursing school in Braddock. Debbie Hines was very supportive and she lived close to our school. I enjoyed visiting with her family. Her mother made the best-ever chili con carne. We became good study buddies, and we stayed in touch for a while after we became professional nurses.

Dixie Smythe came from a family of seven and lived at home during the school semester because it was close by. I enjoyed her large family and spending the night at their house. Since I didn't have multiple siblings or much of a nuclear family where both parents are in harmony, this was an enjoyable experience. I felt like I was part of the family. All of the siblings sat at the table while we ate dinner together. Much laughing and joking went on as Dixie's mom got everyone to be quiet before saying grace. I loved her little sister, who was a toddler at the time. She reminded me of Annmarie. Sensing their camaraderie and cohesiveness was a great opportunity that added to my joy.

Another asset to being on my own at eighteen, while in nursing school, I began writing poetry. To date I have written more than a hundred poems. Haiku is my favorite style. A few of my poems are included as part of this story. Poetry is healing for me. I love the creative process. It is another release of the feelings deep within my soul. I enjoy writing poems for myself and for others, especially for special occasions such as Ricky's and my wedding, anniversaries, achievements, or the loss of a spouse, partner or child.

I have many poignant memories from my time as a nursing student. The most tender one centers on my time with a baby boy with a cleft palate and lip. This infant had his upper lip surgically closed. Later that evening he had no visitors and cried continuously.

Following my care of his dressing change and other physical needs, I carried this child on my shoulder the rest of the evening until he fell asleep while I performed my duties. I felt very connected to him, wanting to give back some of the nurturing I'd received from nurses by providing love and comfort to him. I can still picture this infant as his warm tears and blood-tinged saliva fell on my diaper-covered shoulder. But I didn't care.

During this time, too, I continued to be a regular in the dental chair—for updates, progressive continued care, and for surgeries. I still wore an obturator/prosthesis for speech and for eating and drinking. One surgery smoothed out my lip even more, making my scars less noticeable.

I recognized through these early years of my education that nursing practices would be advanced in the not-too-distant future. It was becoming a reality that nurses needed to have a bachelor's degree in order to practice with confidence and perform effectively in the professional health careers domain. Relevantly, a nurse practitioner—advanced practice registered nurse—certificate program was first developed at the University of Colorado in 1965. Soon, this grew to be a master's of nursing program throughout the country at many colleges and universities. It was introduced to me during my upcoming study of nursing history and theory while I was working on my bachelor of science degree at Duquesne University. It struck my interest and led to the future advancement of my career.

CHAPTER 10:
HAPPY TO BE A
PROFESSIONAL NURSE BUT
DEALING WITH ASSAULT

I graduated from Braddock General Hospital School of Nursing with a nursing diploma in 1972. My class of thirty-one women was followed by the closing of the school due to lack of funding and because nursing education was evolving toward a college education. Within six months, I had successfully passed my state nursing board exam and became a registered nurse. I was so happy to have obtained this professional licensure, a triumph that assisted in raising my self-esteem.

By that time, I knew I wanted to be a nurse practitioner. According to the American Association of Nurse Practitioners, of which I am a member, a nurse practitioner is also known as an advanced practice registered nurse (APRN) and is educated to the masters or doctoral level to provide "primary, acute, chronic, and specialty care to persons of all ages and all walks of life." Later that same year I returned to school to start work on my bachelor of science degree in nursing (BSN) at Duquesne University. I learned that the school of nursing there was very good and they accepted some of my college credits from my diploma school. In addition, I challenged some courses by taking an exam which I passed. I was determined to go on with my education. It took over five years. I started taking evening courses while working full time with the financial assistance of my employer. Then, I began working part-time as I became a full-time student. I was fortunate to be eligible for a nursing traineeship through a federally funded program. This program provided financial support for my education and an allowance during my last year. Thus, maintaining my room and board. I was thankful to complete my courses without having to work for a year.

My next goal was to obtain a driver's license. My mother declined to assist me. That spring, I decided to take a driver's education course in my hometown. It started out fine, the first few weeks my instructor and I were both at the wheel. One evening we were driving down an unfamiliar road. Mr. Fay told me he could make me feel good. All of a sudden, he had a dildo in his hand, which he started stroking up and down my right arm as I was driving. He said, "I can make you feel good." I felt strange and fearful about what was going to happen next. It was getting dark.

My mind and my heart were racing. I knew I had to get out of the car as soon as possible. "I'd like to go home, now." Mr. Fay silently complied and took the dildo away from my arm. I drove as carefully as I could under the circumstances. When I got out of the car, I was trembling.

I got inside the house and told my mother what had just happened, and she said to me, "Go to hell!" I went up to my bedroom and cried. I felt so scared and disgraced. Especially when my mother was so harsh and did not offer to comfort or support me.

Many months later, I saw Mr. Fay playing in a band at a fundraiser. I immediately panicked, trembling and crying. A dear friend, Betsy from my mother's work place, comforted me. I never returned to driver's education with Mr. Fay and did not report him to the authorities. I eventually felt more secure driving with my then-fiancé, John, in the passenger seat. After a time, I obtained my driver's license, but I became so frightened by the police officer during the practical driving part of the test that I had to take it a second time.

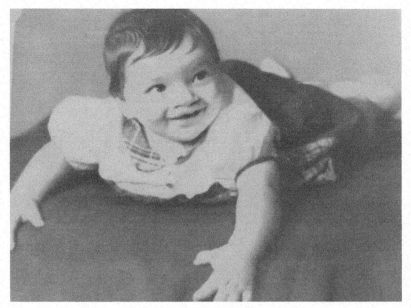

LUCIA AT AGE 6 MONTHS, 1951

LUCIA AT AGE ONE WITH GODMOTHER YOLANDA, 1952

LUCIA AGE 4 AND ANNEMARIE AGE 3, 1955

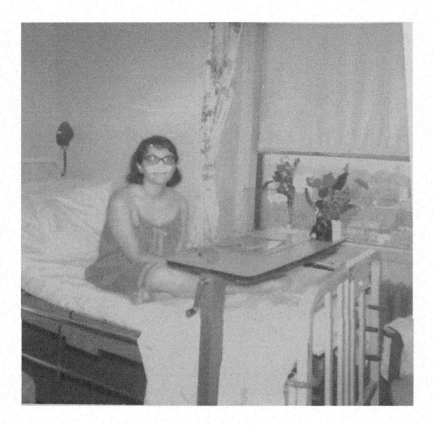

LUCIA AT AGE 17; FOLLOWING NASAL
AND LIP SURGERY, 1968

LUCIA AT AGE 20; GRADUATION FROM BRADDOCK
GENERAL HOSPITAL SCHOOL OF NURSING, 1972

LUCIA AND HER FATHER ANTHONY IN 1972 DURING
HER NURSING SCHOOL GRADUATION PARTY

MARIE ON LUCIA'S 25TH BIRTHDAY, 1976

LUCIA AT AGE 27; RECEIVED HER BACHELOR
OF SCIENCE IN NURSING DEGREE FROM
DUQUESNE UNIVERSITY IN 1978

LEN, MARIE'S BOYFRIEND, LUCIA AND MARIE
AT DUQUESNE UNIVERSITY, 1978

LUCIA AT AGE 37; RECEIVED HER MASTER
OF SCIENCE IN NURSING DEGREE AND
BECAME A FAMILY NURSE PRACTITIONER

LUCIA AND RICKY ON THEIR WEDDING
DAY, FEBRUARY 10, 2000

LUCI RECEIVED HER NEW BRIDGEWORK/
PROSTHESIS ON APRIL 13, 2017

LUCIA AND RICKY AT THEIR NEW HOME; JUNE 3, 2019

LUCIA AND HER DOG, ZOE, APRIL 15, 2020

CHAPTER 11:
ACQUIRING PROFESSIONAL
EXPERIENCE AND
PERSONAL GROWTH

From April to November of 1972 I worked at Braddock General Hospital on a medical–surgical unit. This was my first job as a registered nurse. The first thing I wanted to purchase for myself was contact lenses. I had been wearing eyeglasses since I was eight, and wanted to get rid of them. I was fitted with gas-permeable contact lenses, which I enjoyed wearing for many years. I felt so free at the time and I happily experimented with applying eye make-up without having to think about glasses.

I rented a room in a two-story, five-room house and shared a bathroom and kitchen with a woman named Eileen who had recently become widowed. Eileen was very supportive and became a great friend. I walked to and from work for six months until I saved enough money to put a down payment on my first car. This was a big thrill for me. It was a light yellow, Chevrolet Vega hatchback, just big enough for me. I loved that car.

I then moved on to Montefiore Hospital, a teaching hospital in Pittsburgh with a connection to the University of Pittsburgh. There, I worked on medical–surgical units and in the recovery room, as it was called back then. Today, it is called the post-anesthesia care unit. I had an opportunity to work with both intern and resident physicians. They politely called me the nurse with the crooked smile. My knowledge and experience, as well as my compassion for others, grew and flourished over that five-year period. I was learning so much professionally and how to deal with different personalities. I was given many responsibilities as a young professional nurse. There were some evenings and nights when I was the only registered nurse (RN) on duty on an inpatient unit with up to forty patients, working with one medical assistant and one licensed practical nurse (LPN). I did survive!

It was time to get into my own home, and I informed Eileen of my move in November of 1972. I felt happy having my own one-bedroom apartment, my own car, and the freedom to spend my own money. I started to be proud of my appearance while working, dressing neatly and professionally. My desire was to maintain my professionalism, which continued throughout my career. Over the years, I received compliments from colleagues, coworkers, and patients. This also contributed to my competence and confidence while providing patient care.

I was independent, but I was also in a relationship that I questioned and was drawn to at the same time. He eventually became my husband, and then my former husband, John.

I graduated from Duquesne University in 1978 with a bachelor of science degree in nursing (BSN). At that time, I saw higher education as a ticket to a better life. Earning my degree also gave me a great sense of realization, nurturing my self-esteem. My passion for nursing was endless.

This stretch of nursing was followed by ten years of employment as a visiting nurse, which I qualified for with my BSN. During those years, I worked with a variety of patients with many different illnesses. My work found me caring for a diverse group of adult clients requiring medical–surgical care, renal care, hospice care, and intravenous therapy (IV). I became the IV team supervisor for all of Allegheny County. By then, electronic pumps for IV therapy were being developed and I had the opportunity to learn how to operate a pump and teach others how to use it. I developed a nursing-care plan for IV therapy in the home and gave a presentation in 1982 during an Acquired Immune Deficiency Syndrome (AIDS) conference in Pittsburgh, when I had the good fortune to care for those individuals affected by the disease before plentiful medications were available. Life with this communicable disease was difficult for these clients, due to the lack of treatment at the time. Their immune system was compromised, making them more vulnerable to many disorders and infections. My co-workers and I cared for them until they needed acute hospitalization. This eventually led to these patients' deaths.

The most rewarding part of being a visiting nurse was performing hospice care. Assisting patients to leave the world was a very spiritual, rewarding experience. Dying is as important as being born. I took call and went to their homes in the middle of the night when needed and stayed in touch with the patient's oncologist or other physician. Many of these patients and their families were preparing for their death and appreciated the hospice support. My co-workers and I became part of the family as we made sure the patient was comfortable and peaceful, with minimal pain, as they left the world. Closure, at the funeral home or place of worship, was comforting for the family and for me. The family was thankful for the care their loved one received from us. Being able to die at home was often a blessing. One family was so thankful for our care that they gave a monetary donation to our organization.

Interestingly, my mother questioned my safety when I ventured into the homes of sick people. When there was a question regarding security, such as a patient having a weapon in the home or because the neighborhood was a high-crime area, I had the police escort me or I was accompanied by another nurse. I experienced situations where I called the county health department due to poor living conditions, such as lack of proper plumbing or toilet use. I dealt with mice, roaches, maggots, and filth. Fortunately, I experienced no harm doing this in-home nursing work.

One time I was in the hospital following surgery to restore the bony ridge height of my upper teeth. Unable to eat or drink by mouth, I had a flexible, soft rubber nasogastric feeding tube in place that went from my nose down into my stomach. The tube was attached to an electric pump.

When the nurses were busy, I was able to disconnect and reconnect my own feeding tube to the pump if I wanted to walk to the bathroom. They appreciated that I could do that and I felt confident and skillful.

I continued to enjoy nursing and to receive care from a prosthodontist and a general dentist. My prosthesis was being maintained. Fortunately, the Bureau of Vocational Rehabilitation assisted me again with associated costs, so I could maintain my profession.

CHAPTER 12:
STRESSFUL
FAMILY COMMUNICATION

In 1979, I married a man who had been one of my hospital patients. He had a kidney stone. We met while I was working at my first job on a medical–surgical unit at the hospital where I had graduated. I gave him an enema without any thought. It was part of my job. We joked about it for a while and then stopped talking about it.

I was attracted to this man by his caring way and his ability to give me the attention I craved from a man. We dated for seven years before marrying. We enjoyed going to the movies, going out to dinner and spending time with friends and family. Looking back, it was too long. I gave him an ultimatum to either marry or not and did not stick to it. I even broke off with him and dated another man I met at my work and then ended up going back to him. This marriage was a stepping-stone for my personal growth. I was seeking the father that I felt I had lost. John was fourteen years my senior. He was supportive at the beginning of our courtship and marriage. We traveled to Florida and to Canada and enjoyed going to refurbished antique car shows. He even helped me with making copies of my school papers while I was working on my bachelor of science in nursing degree and respected my need to complete my necessary homework without interruption.

In addition, he had a very close relationship with his mother, which I didn't see as a red flag. During our wedding reception, my mother and my new mother-in-law got into a heated argument about the gifts we had received, which resulted in my mother phoning us during our honeymoon and yelling at us. We suffered with that huge insult. This fiasco felt like another, even larger, red flag for our relationship.

My mother in-law, Mae depended on John, her youngest son, more than her other three children and her husband. He was with her when she died in the hospital with heart problems. The hospital personnel thought they were husband and wife.

My elderly father -in-law, Jim, had developed Alzheimer's Disease. He became confused and disoriented, and died in their home. I had an opportunity to care for him before his passing.

In 1984, after years of not seeing my father, I made the decision to pursue a reunion with him. I searched for and found him. I wrote him a letter, asking him why he had ceased contact with me during my childhood. He wrote back, stating that when my mother and I moved away from our last home together as a family, he went to my school to find me. He reported finding only an old address, from which my mother, her boyfriend, and I had already moved.

There was a gap of information about the other places where we lived. My father stated that we moved again and then he could not find me. He reported that he did not stop loving me and was proud of me and apologized for not being present during my childhood. Explaining that life is hard for some people, he gave me his full address and phone number. I visited him at his residence in my hometown, which he shared with a woman and two other men. I don't remember all the details and if he was still employed. Not much was said about it.

I was so excited to see my daddy. I was just happy to be with him and to embrace him and, at the same time, felt strange about being away from each other for many years. He appeared to be well, smiling as we spoke. He told me that he was proud of me and my career. We had a nice visit and an exchange of pictures. And he met John. My father alluded that I would take care of him when the time came. I felt that I couldn't do that with our lack of relationship all those years.

I told my mother about it before the visit and she became uneasy and angry. "Why do you want to do that?" I explained it was something I needed to do.

CHAPTER 13:
CREATING CONNECTION
AND SUPPORT

When I was twenty, I saw a plastic surgeon who told me that nothing else could be done for me. This incident spurred me to pursue the attention I deserved at the maxillofacial clinic at the University of Pittsburgh. There I met a speech therapist who was very supportive. Ali B. provided love, encouragement, friendship, and good therapeutic advice.

For years, I had wondered why my mother and other family members such as my aunts, uncles, and cousins didn't talk about my birth defect. I felt a need to talk to others with similar issues and get their input. I wanted to talk about my facial difference and support other women and parents of affected children, people of all ages.

Ali encouraged me to be my best self and assisted me in creating a support group in 1983 called Looking Ahead, co-created with two other women with facial difference, Linda and Rhonda. We gathered and shared data for the group from a social worker at the clinic with respect to privacy.

The group grew to seven women and one man with facial difference from the metropolitan area. We all had goals and aspirations. We had monthly meetings at each other's homes and occasionally had guest speakers from the university. We talked about our past and present lives and issues, such as one husband telling his wife he was tired of looking at her facial scars and wanted a divorce; another husband requested his wife get an abortion due to fear of having a child with the same issues, which she regretted doing; and a grandfather telling one member of our group that no man would want her; parents holding back a college education due to a member's image; fear of rejection by another member's family who her sent away to live with her grandparents on their farm, due solely to her appearance.

These are a few examples of our conversations: being labeled by parents and teachers as having less intelligence because of our birth defect, feeling alienated, feeling afraid of kissing, enduring low self-esteem, and, of course, navigating relationship issues. We discussed our positive surgery outcomes, make-up application tips to cover our scars, validated our sensitivities, and admitted to over compensating to be our best despite our facial difference. Sharing personal experiences at the end of each meeting enlightened me and awakened me to the fact that I was not alone on my journey.

Linda shared about her fear of driving in traffic and not receiving her driver's license until she turned thirty due to her appearance from the side. Rhonda shared her story of being on a date. When she declined to have sex with her date, he called her "Snub Nose Thirty-Eight." Other names mentioned were "Snot Lip" and "Lemon Lip."

A success story came out of this group. We had one young man, Daniel, who was a violinist for the symphony. He would not sit in the front row due to his facial difference and grew a mustache to hide the scars on his upper lip. After attending our meetings, he was easily able to sit in the front row without his mustache and without apprehension. It was great knowing our group made a difference!

The support group lasted for about two years, eventually folding due to lack of attendance. It was one of the best things I ever did for myself, enriching my continuous healing. I gained so much camaraderie, friendship, and knowledge. The group is an uplifting and enduring memory that will be with me forever.

CHAPTER 14:
AN ABUSIVE MARRIAGE

As I grew professionally, my husband became emotionally and physically abusive. Our fourteen-year age difference did not help. He declined to maintain employment as a dispatcher at the railroad and was struggling with his family relationships. At the time, the steel mills were in the process of shutting down. This affected his job that served the steel mills.

In 1985, I initiated psychological counseling to address my cleft lip and palate, but soon found myself discussing my relationship with my husband. The process of delving into my feelings, self-worth, and emotions was very helpful, assisting me in making future decisions and in reshaping my life. It was one of the best decisions I ever made. I remained in counseling for many years.

John was angry and frustrated. He verbally belittled me by calling me "bitch" or "whore" and tried to control me by telling me what to do and wear. And when I disagreed with him, he put me down even more. He called my graduate school classes "Phi Zappa Crappa." I was in the process of expanding my career and this man was struggling with his own demons, not doing anything about his own life or his employment. I actually felt that he was jealous of me and he was lazy. Looking back, I know he needed help regarding his abusive behavior.

My counselor at the time described his behavior as that of a fourteen-year-old teenager. John told me that if we ever had children, he would turn them against me. In addition, when I was working as an intravenous supervisor for the Visiting Nurses Association and one of my team nurses called me for assistance, he told them not to call and bother me. I had no idea this was happening until years later.

I walked on eggshells, living in fear. One day he broke a window in our dining room. Another evening he stepped hard on my toes. Fortunately, I did not endure a serious injury. I called the local police and nothing was done because the situation was not taken seriously. Today, this incident would be defined as domestic violence.

I decided it was time to make another change in my life. One activity got me through this stressful time. I performed or taught aerobic dance nearly six days a week. It was during one of these classes that my engagement ring fell off my finger, never to be found. No one at my aerobic studio turned in the ring. I saw this as an omen to my future in this relationship.

In 1986, I had another major surgery completed by Doctor George S. to correct the misalignment of my upper and lower jaws, which affected my bite. My upper jaw, called the maxilla, was therapeutically broken and reset. I came home with my jaws wired shut and a temporary metal appliance in place over my missing hard and soft palates in order to keep the upper jaw separated to facilitate the restorative process. It was a time to make a liquid diet tasty. My blender became my friend. What a way to lose weight! Thankfully, it was only a short time before I could again eat solid food. The ten pounds I lost returned when I went back to eating solid foods. This successful surgery became a stepping-stone toward my next major surgery.

In July of 1987, while in graduate school, I filed for divorce. I felt unsafe in my home and knew it was time to leave. John made it difficult for me when he received the list of belongings I was requesting, through his lawyer, to take with me. He blocked me from parking my car in the garage on subzero winter nights. He told his family that I was unfaithful, which was untrue.

My female lawyer, Gwendolyn, was my champion. By November of the same year, my divorce became final. Surprisingly, it took only four months. Gwendolyn congratulated me by giving me back my maiden name—without charge. I will never forget her and her gift. It was great to see it on my diploma when I received my master's degree.

The day I moved into my new apartment; John attempted to destroy the furniture by breaking the glass top of my bedroom dresser. My mother, godmother, and two very good friends, Lynn and Jane, were with me that day. I have always felt grateful for their presence.

My mother purchased curtains for my large patio window and door, which was very helpful. I felt peace and serenity in my new home. It was like a cocoon.

However, one day I saw John while driving in traffic. He was headed in the opposite direction; still, I began to panic, fearing he would come after me. Luckily, he drove on. I was so relieved.

Many years later, in 1993, I had my marriage annulled in the Catholic church. My former husband did not participate in the process, making the task easier to achieve.

During the years following my divorce, I read many self-help books about toxic relationships, melancholy, co-dependency, self-nurturing, and self-care. I also enjoyed philosophy and spiritual readings. I was on a path to self-actualization and never gave up. I gravitated toward people who were supportive and loving. I refused to think of my birth defect as a disability. I attended psychotherapy regularly. My therapist told me that I was tenacious.

Encouraged by my therapist, I wrote a letter to John—that I did not send to him—to release my feelings. I told him that he took advantage of my low self-esteem and I hated him for that. I stated that I didn't need a perfectionist, domineering bastard like him causing me apprehension and vigilance and that I deserved a loving, trusting, and healthy relationship. Writing the letter was very palliative and beneficial.

I returned to dance classes of all kinds: tap, ballroom, ballet, aerobics, flamenco, and jazz. As mentioned earlier, dance was always a healing factor for me. I felt so light and free to be myself. I have pursued dance classes intermittently throughout my adult life, mainly tap, ballet, and aerobics.

CHAPTER 15:
ADDITIONAL OPPORTUNITIES,
A DREAM COME TRUE, AND
HALLMARK SURGERY!

Many opportunities opened up for me. I spoke on the phone to other adults with clefts anticipating surgery about my own experience with maxillofacial surgery and spoke to a group of medical students at the University of Pittsburgh School of Medicine about my personal restorative history. I had the pleasure of being a model one day for a make-up line that minimized facial scars. These activities gave me real positive feelings about myself.

In 1984, I had attempted to enter the Family Nurse Practitioner program at the University of Pittsburgh. My goal was to attend this program and I knew it was the one for me. I made an appointment to see the director of the program following my workday at the Visiting Nurses Association of Allegheny County. Wearing my navy-blue uniform, I entered her office. She was obese, smoking a cigarette, and drinking a can of soda.

Ms. Price told me I wouldn't make it and turned me away. I persevered and returned in 1986, telling the same director to let me in—and she did. I wrote an essay of intent that was convincing.

What followed was two years of intense studies and practicums. The first year I worked full time and took evening classes. The second year I qualified for a federally funded nursing traineeship, again. It gave me the opportunity to not work that year and complete my graduate program. Luckily, I received monies from my former home during my divorce to support myself. I graduated in December of 1988 from the University of Pittsburgh with my master of science in nursing degree as a family nurse practitioner. I can't describe my joy at this accomplishment. I had dreamed about it for years. Suddenly, here it was. My dream had come true!

The amazing part is that I went through with the divorce, packed up the house, and relocated, all while in graduate school—and made it! I was inducted into the National Honor Society for Nursing. My mother, godmother, and two dear friends, Lynn and Emma, were warmly supportive during this time. Their encouragement made my transition easier. I am so appreciative.

My mother and godmother, Yolanda, and my dear friends stayed with me the whole day following the graduation ceremony, which actually took place in May of 1989. I told my mother I didn't want a party. I felt like I did not want to be patronized by her. Just a quiet dinner at one of my favorite restaurants would be fine. We enjoyed a delicious Italian dinner at the historic Pleasure Bar in Pittsburgh, which just happened to be a restaurant with a bar. I enjoyed the togetherness as we celebrated my success.

Following completion of my graduate degree, right after Christmas, I underwent a major, hallmark surgery as my way of bringing in the New Year. My pharyngeal flap was constructed by a renowned Pittsburgh plastic surgeon, Doctor William G. He took the pharyngeal muscle in the back of my throat, which helps us swallow, and sliced it from ear to ear, just enough to cover my hard and soft palate openings, relieving me from having to wear an obturator anymore. He even made me a uvula—the small, fleshy, teardrop-shaped tissue projecting down from the middle of the soft palate. I was so thrilled! This surgery was not available in the 1950s when I was an infant. An amazing outcome followed the surgery: My speech was perfect because of the skill of my plastic surgeon and my efforts to speak eloquently.

Several weeks following the surgery, my prosthodontist, Doctor Hussein Z. gave me the privilege of throwing my obturator into the trash. I took it into my hand, happily stretching out my arm as I tossed it away. It was my vital buddy for many years that temporarily restored my soft and hard palates and my front teeth. What a momentous time for me! I shed many tears of joy during this short, emotional ceremony. This was another turning point on my journey. I did wear a temporary set of frontal false teeth until my next major surgery

To this day, the pharyngeal flap works well for me. The only drawback is I have a very small opening, called a fistula, adjacent to my right frontal canine tooth, which is the pointy one. I have tiny leaks of fluid and wet food go up into my, nose causing me to sneeze. This does not occur often and is nothing compared to having a wide-open cleft palate. An attempt to close the fistulas in 1990 failed, which I accepted.

CHAPTER 16:
EVOLUTION AND INCREASED
SELF AWARENESS

My first position as a nurse practitioner in 1989 was working at the Veteran's Administration Medical Center ambulatory, diabetic clinic. I managed about 300 diabetics. Three of them were women and the remaining were men. My job included treatment of their diabetes with physical exams, prescribing oral medications and insulin, referring them to specialists such as podiatry, ophthalmology, and nephrology, and educating them and their families and friends about self-monitoring of their blood sugars at home, dietary guidance, and how to inject insulin. I thoroughly enjoyed this rewarding job. These jovial men brought me all kinds of gifts from doughnuts to jewelry to wine. My most cherished gift is a lapel pin of the American flag, which I continue to treasure.

Later, due to professional difficulty with a nurse practitioner colleague, Karen, who also worked in the clinic, I chose to transfer and work in the geriatric clinic. Sweetly, my veteran clients continued to seek my care.

Another goal I set for myself was to communicate to the public the role of the nurse practitioner, to call attention to our value in various areas of health care such as primary care, internal medicine, and medical specialties such as pediatrics, dermatology, gastroenterology, oncology, and women's health.

From 1992 to 1995 I was featured in many newspapers, including the *Pennsylvania Nurse*, *The Kansas City Star*, *The Kansas City Nursing News*, and the *Cass County Democrat Missourian*. I was very proud of my primary care practice, supporting my clients of all ages, being their advocate and making sure they received safe and competent care with regard to medications, education, and self-care. These articles included part of my story. In addition, I shared my poetry with my clients and colleagues. I know what it is like to be a patient on the other side of the hospital bed. Knowing about my background felt reassuring to my clients.

CHAPTER 17:
LIFE AS A SINGLE WOMAN,
GAINING FORTITUDE

In the latter part of 1989, two years after my divorce, I decided to get into the dating scene. I began attending singles dances and I had a fun time meeting new people. One gentleman became my dance partner and we hit it off. We began dating. Tim was very loving, supportive, and tender. We dated for nearly four years. We became more serious. He proposed, but I declined due to his living with his mother at age forty. I didn't want history to repeat itself. The year following our breakup, he purchased his own home. In 2016, I found out from his sister, Mary, that he had died at age fifty-nine from complications of Parkinson's disease. In 2017, I went to his gravesite with my husband, Ricky, and two of my friends from Pittsburgh, Lynn and Tina. I will never forget this gentleman who was the first man to come into my life following my divorce. My friend Ali described Tim as "comfortable as an old shoe."

In early 1991, I found out I needed another major surgery. The top portion of my right hip, called the iliac crest bone, was harvested to give me a premaxilla bone—the middle upper jawbone—where our front teeth attach. It is called an alveolar bone graft.

This was done in order to support dental implants. Two titanium rods were installed into the new premaxilla in order to hold them in place, along with capped teeth. Unfortunately, one implant fell out two weeks later. The other one was left in place in order for me to have prosthetic front teeth, also called a bridge. Due to this failure, the titanium implant was not reinstalled. A bridge with four false teeth was then attached to the one existing implant. More stress was placed on my existing upper teeth toward the front of my mouth. My prosthodontist, Doctor Hussein, was able to make it work by taking impressions and the intricate process of having it made in a special laboratory for molding. I was able to eat soft food and progress to regular food, being careful not to bite into anything with my front teeth. My smile returned after the bridge was completed and the front teeth were in place. In fact, the post-operative pain I experienced was more in my right hip than in my mouth. I had difficulty walking for a few weeks. This bridge with the false teeth lasted for many years.

My next practitioner assignment was in internal medicine and occupational health. I learned so much from this experience, from both the physicians and my nurse practitioner colleagues. I greatly enjoyed using the microscope to diagnose urinary and vaginal infections with the assistance of Doctor Sean. I took care of those with acute and chronic medical problems, performed occupational exams and immigration exams, performed phlebotomy, urine drug testing, hearing, and vision testing, as well as spirometry (breath) testing. Of course, I prescribed medications.

Since I was single, with nothing holding me in Pittsburgh, I decided to relocate to California. I applied for and received my professional California nursing license, but a position did not pop up for me at that time. The jobs were not anything I was interested in. So, I decided to wait.

In 1994, a recruiter from Kansas City contacted me and convinced me to travel there for an interview for a position in family practice in a rural area of Missouri. I ended up taking the position. I had the opportunity to treat all age groups, from infancy to geriatrics. This job was very rewarding and my supervising physician–mentor opened my professional horizons to include pediatrics. I had avoided working with children because of my childhood bullying history. This experience helped dissipate that fear. My comfort level performing primary care for children soared. I am forever grateful to Doctor Dillon for his support.

One great aspect about this job is that I was recognized as the first nurse practitioner in Cass County, Missouri. I was acknowledged as a pioneer by my then-nursing supervisor, Jean, who hired more nurse practitioners to come to this underserved area of the state.

In 1995, my mother informed me that my father had died of a heart attack. Because we had not had a relationship for several years, I could not bring myself to attend his funeral. I felt that closure of our relationship had taken place years earlier. We each contributed to a lack of connection. I didn't communicate with my father after 1984, and neither did he with me. I continued to think about the lost relationship that could have existed for years while I was growing up. Not knowing he was living in my hometown all along was disheartening, and I was sad every year on Father's Day, not being with him.

Since I was a single woman, I chose to live in Kansas City, traveling to and from my work in two different towns. The commute became taxing during the blustery winter months, but I enjoyed living in the area, acquiring new friends, and enjoying blues and jazz music, history, and the great barbecued food. After three years, I changed to working at an internal medicine practice closer to my home.

After settling in, I joined a few dating services (before Internet dating) and met some interesting men who didn't work out. They were not yet over their previous relationships or didn't want to spend any money on a date. I did meet one gentleman, Dennis, who was fun and attentive. We traveled to Branson, Missouri, Eureka Springs, Arkansas, and other places. Dennis was very caring following one of my upper-lip surgeries, assisting me with wound care. The relationship lasted for about four years, until I found out he had been unfaithful. This was troubling for me. I felt crushed for several months. I returned to the dating service and did not meet anyone else I was interested in for an ongoing relationship.

During this time, I joined a singles organization with several subgroups through the Village Presbyterian Church in Prairie Village, Kansas. A poetry group met every week, and I had the opportunity to share my poems. In fact, we put on a reading for the single people in the community.

In addition, the poetry group came together and had a book of our poems published called *To Know Thyself, Book II*. Three of my poems are in the book. I proudly gave a copy to my mother and she was impressed.

CHAPTER 18:

EXPANDING SPIRITUALITY

Another interest came into my life in 1998. I began meditation and Reiki classes. My instruction and practice grew to the point of my becoming a third-degree Reiki Master in 2005. There are four levels. The word Reiki means universal life energy. It is hands-on healing energy and was developed by Dr. Usui Mikao in the mid 1860s in Kyoto, Japan. Through many following masters, it made its way to America (Rand, 2000, 1-15). Reiki is not a religion and it is not a cure, but a reflective and blissful presence. I have been practicing intermittently for years.

This soothing energy touch has brought me into connection with my soul, as it works on the energy centers of the body, called *chakras*. Chakras are circles of life energy that run from the bottom of the spinal cord up to the crown of the head. Each chakra has its own color and distinguishing characteristics associated with physical, mental, and spiritual communications.

My desire now is to totally get back into this rewarding practice for myself and with others.

Today, Reiki is offered in medical facilities and in hospice programs. There has been ongoing research done on the effectiveness of the practice, and it continues to be efficacious for patients in reducing anxiety and depression and in lowering blood pressure. It assists those with acute and chronic disease, terminal illness, and eases pain (McManus, 2017, 1051-1057).

In addition, I began Yoga instruction in Kansas City. I have tried different types over the years and continue to practice regularly. Yoga is another great de-stressor and calming practice for me. I enjoy the meditation at the end of each class and the loving energy. It brings balance to my core and has become an important part of my life.

CHAPTER 19:
MY NEW HUSBAND AND
NEW ADVENTURES

In 1999, I decided to join one last dating service called Together. I had a few dates and then I met Ricky. We exchanged background information. Then we got together on the phone. After a long and pleasant conversation, we had our first date at a local Mexican restaurant, followed by a movie. We continued to date and enjoy one another's company. I met his family and his four children living nearby, Allen, Stella, Matthew and Nicholas and he eventually met my mother. We knew we were in love after the first few weeks.

We married seven months later in February, while on a nurse practitioner continuing education cruise in the Caribbean. During our second port of call, we were married on the beach at Magen's Bay, St. Thomas Island, in our bathing suits. I wore a red tankini, a pareo, and a crown of white flowers and carried a bouquet of identical flowers. It was the most beautiful ceremony. We wrote our own vows and danced to the song, *Grow Old Along with Me*, sung by Mary Chapin Carpenter and written by John Lennon. Ricky carried me into the ocean without dropping me!

We had a celebration for family and friends when we returned home and requested everyone wear beach clothing. We had a beach theme with fake palm trees and lovely handheld fans for everyone. It was a fun celebration of our marriage. We had the opportunity to perform the dance we learned from our ballroom dance instructor—the foxtrot—with the music performed by our friend and gifted harpist, Paula. It was a magical day!

On occasion we joke about being Ricky and Lucy from the television show, *I Love Lucy*. Ricky will sometimes call out when he gets into the front door of our home, "Lucy, I'm home!"

We settled into our new home in Kansas City. At that time, I was still working in internal medicine. Shortly thereafter I lost my job due to downsizing, and their offer to have me stay and work part time would not support me financially. I decided to accept a position and teach at Research College of Nursing in Kansas City in the undergraduate and graduate programs and work part time at an internal medicine practice in order to maintain my primary-care skills.

Another opportunity came up for me while working in internal medicine. I saw women of all ages with healthcare issues centered on their reproductive organs. I was big on providing education for self-care of this vital system. Many women douched and developed heightened inflammatory problems, so I wrote and developed an educational handout titled "The Perils of Vaginal Douching."

This short essay made it to an online source called www.mum. org, the website for the Museum of Menstruation and Women's Health. The website addresses the history of menstruation and women's health for lay people and healthcare professionals. Much-needed information has been provided by that website, and it continues to be available. My essay was published on that site in 2000 and was copyrighted by the founder of the museum, Mr. Harry Finley, to whom I am eternally appreciative. The essay has been recognized by international medical resources as valuable information.

During this time, my restorative prosthetic device failed. The single existing titanium implant developed an infection and fell out. The bone was even more depleted. This resulted in my needing to have another permanent frontal prothesis/bridge of teeth be made by my next prosthodontist, Doctor Gidman. It was processed similarly to the previous one. False teeth were attached to match my existing teeth, which were capped with specific metal to be made stronger. This would again restore my lost bone and teeth.

The bridge was bonded to my existing teeth. It was larger than the previous bridge, but I was able to adapt to it. My teeth did not show as much when I smiled. I was able to tolerate it and it did work for me for many years. The process did not interfere with my work schedule. However, it was emotional for me because through it I remembered my journey and the pain I had endured with regard to previous dental work and surgeries.

During the summer of 2001, Ricky and I attended Ricky's family reunion in Estes Park, near Rocky Mountain National Park in Colorado. We enjoyed the beauty of that natural and beautiful environment. Ricky was ready to leave his heating, air conditioning, and ventilation business and I was ready for a change. His adult children were doing well. So, we decided to move to Loveland, Colorado. Because nurse practitioner positions were few and far between, I began a Reiki practice that was rewarding for my clients and myself, but not lucrative enough.

In 2002, I underwent two more surgeries in Kansas City. In April, before we moved, I had my last rhinoplasty (nose job) with reshaping of my nostrils, lip revision on both sides, and refurbishment of the right side of the bony ridge height of my upper teeth. I was happy with this surgery. The scars on my upper lip appeared less obvious. My nose remained slightly distorted, but nothing more could be done for it. This was fine with me.

I returned with Doctor John H. one last time in October 2002 for lip-plumping surgery for better balance. He made me a Cupid's bow. Separate areas of lip tissue were brought together toward the center of the mouth, providing a heart shape to the upper lip that resembled the bow of Cupid, the Roman god of love (Gallagher, and medically reviewed by Cynthia Cobb, DNP, APRN, 2020). The results gave me an exciting reason to start wearing lipstick!

These last two surgeries were the final ones of approximately thirty-four. I was finally done! Doctor John was so caring. I will always be indebted to him.

In 2004, I found a position in radiation/oncology for a year as a registered nurse because I could not secure a nurse practitioner position. I then returned to working in endocrinology, caring for diabetics while in Denver, and in gastroenterology in Lafayette and Boulder, Colorado. I gained more knowledge and widened my experience, and I met many remarkable people. Unfortunately, I was later laid off due to the medical director of the practice wanting to hire more physicians. The practice decided not to utilize the skills of nurse practitioners at that time.

CHAPTER 20:
THE LOSS OF MY MOTHER
AND AN ATTITUDE CHANGE

My mother died in 2004 from multiple organ failure and a stroke. Her death took place at the inpatient hospice house in our hometown, for which she had helped raise construction funds. It was a time of mourning for me, because her passing brought up a deep grief for what had always been lacking in our relationship. Nonetheless, I came away from that grief thankful for what we did have and for what my mother taught me over the years, such as independence and self-sufficiency. I remember her telling me, "Once you made a decision to do something, you always completed your task." I also told her not to feel guilty about my birth defect. This connection brought added harmony to our relationship.

My mother had been an active volunteer with the March of Dimes, a nonprofit, eighty-one-year-old organization with a role to reduce birth defects by supporting the prenatal care and health of mothers and babies (2019). She led fundraising walkathons and other events in the community to raise funds for this worthy cause. She never talked to me about why she did it. However, my speculation is that was her way of dealing with her two daughters being born with birth defects and the terrible loss of losing one daughter. Her volunteerism over the years was much appreciated by the community, and I have kept some of her award plaques.

As mentioned previously, for years I had seen my hometown as a dark and depressing place, given my many negative memories from there that outweighed positive ones. Once I became a professional nurse, I vowed never to live there again. My visits there were short. As soon as I arrived, I was ready to leave.

In the mid 1990s, after doing much spiritual and emotional work, my thoughts turned to seeing my hometown as just another place to visit. This was a great accomplishment for me. Coming to this acceptance, I felt so free. A dark cloud was lifted. This was an attitude change!

I visited my mother on both special and necessary occasions. I returned every two years to visit my valued cousins and friends in my hometown of Washington and my dear friends in Pittsburgh. I will never forget my cousin, Angelo. His generosity and thoughtfulness impressed me. He offered his restaurant space and provided delicious food for my mother's post-funeral luncheon. He created a welcoming space for people to feel free to stand up and honor my mother with a short speech. I, meanwhile, had her photos and memorabilia of her accomplishments on display nearby.

Since my mother's passing, I have continued to visit Washington and Pittsburgh. I enjoy seeing my surviving family members and friends, especially Angelo, Stephanie, and Lynn. I also check on the cemetery where my parents and sister are buried, as I reflect on my cherished memories. I make sure the burial sites and stones are intact and not in need of service.

Adding yet another therapeutic practice, I have journaled since 1989. In 2003, I decided to amend my practice by writing down five things to be grateful for every night before going to sleep. I believe this practice has been very grounding and therapeutic, another aid to my persistent and balanced recovery. It continues today and has become my nightly ritual.

CHAPTER 21:
BUTTERFLIES AND JOY

Another aspiration has brought me many pleasant memories. I wanted to raise butterflies and create a butterfly farm. So, I did some research and decided to purchase some Painted Ladies caterpillars. They stayed in a plastic shoebox with holes in the top and I placed food on the lid for them to eat. Their job was to eat a lot of food while I cleaned up their droppings. Once they got fat, they then transformed into chrysalises, which were hard shelled, hanging from the lid of the box. When all the chrysalises were formed, I hung them inside the wall of a cardboard box that I placed in a mesh cage. Within a week, the butterflies emerged. Liquid color from their wings dropped onto the floor of the box when they stretched out their wings. I shed tears seeing my butterflies. I then removed the cardboard box so they could fly freely about the cage. They began mating at the top of the cage almost immediately.

One butterfly was deformed, with curled wings, and when it tried to elevate itself it fell back down repeatedly. With empathy, I watched it saunter around the cage.

Interestingly, there was one chrysalis that did not open for several days, so I placed it in the garage trashcan. One day, I went out to the garage and saw a butterfly flying around. Since she had been in the trash, I decided to release her so she would not infect the other butterflies in the cage. I went outside a few days later to find she had returned to her home, and was on the driveway. This was so touching for me!

These butterflies lived for two to six weeks, sustained on milkweed. When there were a few left, I released them. I had done much reading, and had met and spoken with butterfly farmers at their organizational conference in Florida. I decided raising butterflies was not for me. Yet my experience brought me rich joy and an appreciation for these colorful creatures known as flying flowers, taken from the original Greek word for butterfly, *petaluthas*.

Butterflies have been my totem creature for years. The butterfly is a symbol of perseverance, transformation, hope, joy, and life—a reflection of my journey. They can be found in my home in many forms, and I usually have a butterfly bush in my garden so they will come and visit during the warmer months of the year. I greatly cherish them. Give me anything with butterflies on it or in it and I am delighted!

CHAPTER 22:
A RESEARCH PROJECT
AND FUN WITH HORSES

In 2005, Ricky and I moved to Parker, Colorado. I became a part-time senior professional research assistant at the University of Colorado at Denver Health and Sciences Center, School of Pharmacy for a year. My duties included taking medical histories, performing physical exams, monitoring laboratory work, and monitoring all research participants throughout a double-blind study of a drug used for diabetes on those without diabetes. The research participants had no knowledge if they had taken the real drug or a sugar pill until the research project was completed. Angie, my supervisor and the chief investigator and pharmacist, was researching how people respond to this particular drug based on genetic makeup. The outcome of the study was published and I am listed as one of the authors.

Following the study, I became a clinical and classroom instructor at Regis University in Denver and performed primary care at a retail medicine clinic. Teaching adult students in the classroom was very challenging. Some conveyed an attitude of privilege, wanting test answers be given to them, unwilling to do the required work to succeed on their own in the nursing profession. This was a great learning experience for me, which I was glad to depart.

A joyful endeavor for me was beginning horseback riding lessons in rural Colorado at a therapeutic riding ranch. This was a soothing activity for me that had been on my bucket list. My love and respect for horses increased as I gained riding skill, guiding the horse to where I wanted it to go. I may return to it someday.

I assisted with therapeutic riding for disabled children and performed first aid on my female mare, Star. She had a gaping wound on her hip following a run-in with a tree branch. I cleansed her wound until the veterinarian arrived. My wound care was so gentle, she did not flinch.

On another occasion, my instructor, Rita's, toddler granddaughter, Amy, needed a post-operative dressing of her hand and fingers changed because it kept falling off. I showed them a figure-eight dressing to help it stay in place for a longer period of time. They were appreciative. This time was also gratifying and valuable for me.

CHAPTER 23:
A MOVE TO CALIFORNIA AND
CAREER ADVANCEMENT

In 2008, Ricky and I decided to venture to northern California, which became favorable for both of us. I had always wanted to come to the state and my professional license was on file there, it just needed to be activated. We moved to the Central Valley. I had several professional appointments there through a recruiter and, after much consideration, I decided to become a psychiatric mental health nurse practitioner. San Joaquin County Behavioral Health was generous enough to hire me as their first nurse practitioner. I agreed to pursue a post-graduate certificate at the University of California, Fresno. It was an intense program, especially since I was working full time. The beauty of this time was twofold. I was able to perform my practicum while on the job, and Ricky was supportive as househusband. He took care of our household tasks, for which I am forever grateful.

I graduated from the program and became nationally certified via exam by the American Nurses Association Credentialing Center (ANCC). I feel proud that I was also certified by the ANCC as a family nurse practitioner. I am forever thankful for my mentoring psychiatrist, Doctor Bart, who guided and supported me from the very beginning. He has a special place in my heart. My initial orientation training started with the inpatient psychiatric health facility where I had the opportunity to observe and interact with the severely mentally ill. This was an informative eye opener for me.

The program helped me to advance my skills in psychiatry, to further understand the complexity of psychiatric pharmacotherapy, and understand and appreciate the minds of the mentally ill and those struggling with illicit and prescription drug use.

The next eight and a half years were filled with caring for the mentally ill, using my skills to manage my caseload of adult clients in the community adult treatment center, plus clients coming to the adult ambulatory setting in the crisis department and in the twenty-three-hour crisis stabilization unit. This included involuntary and voluntary admissions. We offered acute care for mental health emergencies, providing urgent medication injections as needed as well as oral medications, medical care, and consultation with the nursing staff when necessary. Physical exams were completed on clients in restraints. My heart went out to these individuals, even when they were violent or manipulative. With gratitude, I received two awards for my exemplary care and service to the community.

CHAPTER 24:
A LOOK INTO MY CULTURE

In 2011, Ricky and I embarked on a three-week tour of Italy. We took a few side trips beyond the tour. The first side trip was driving to Lake Como and Mandello Del Lario. While there, we enjoyed a fabulous lunch of wood-fired pizza and red wine, appreciating the beautiful vistas out over the lake. We enjoyed a tour of the Moto Guzzi Motorcycle Museum and factory, which Ricky loved. Another adventure was traveling to the Campania area of Italy, to a small, hilly town called Aquara. There, we were shown the birth records of both of my paternal grandparents, which we photographed. That was the highlight of our trip. The people were warm and welcoming. My maiden last name was listed among others on the town square's pillars.

The next adventure was taking a train from Sorrento to Palermo, Sicily. It was exciting when our train car was placed on a barge to the island. Our visit to Termini Immerse was fun because we felt relaxed, not rushed as on the tour. We took our time walking around the town and viewing the panoramic Mediterranean Sea. I was also seeking my maternal grandparents' roots, but without success, even with the help of the staff of the local town hall. Nonetheless, experiencing the food and meeting the people made the day delightful. The Mediterranean was calm and picturesque. The town hall staff gave me a colorful commemorative book that celebrated the town and the many fish in that sea; it contained many photographs. Written in Italian, it is, however, a cherished memento. My culture has been a gift in so many ways. I am thankful my grandparents ventured to America as immigrants to make a better life for themselves and their families, which includes me.

CHAPTER 25:
A NEW PROSTHESIS AND A
BEAUTIFUL, IMPERFECT SMILE

In 2014, my prosthetic device/bridge of fourteen years was cracking along my right front incisor tooth. My general dentist referred me to a prosthodontist, Doctor Craig W. in Rocklin, California. Due to my missing frontal bone and teeth, Doctor Craig worked hard to convince Ricky and me that I needed to have much work done. My issue was presented as restorative — to aid in daily function related to eating, drinking, speech, and being face to face with people at work. After many months of writing to, talking with, and appealing to local and state representatives, my major medical insurance agreed to cover the cost and dental insurance was put in place to cover my remaining needs. My prosthodontist was very supportive, advocating my case to a managing dentist representative at my major medical insurance company, emphasizing my need for functionality with regard to my daily performance.

It took nearly three years and many visits with Doctor Craig to get the restorative work completed, the delay due to insurance issues and other issues with the laboratory that constructed my new prosthesis/bridge. The end result contributed to my self-confidence. My smile was wide, with shiny teeth! I am endlessly appreciative to Doctor Craig.

My detailed oral hygiene habit continues every day. I use an electric toothbrush and water pick two times a day. I floss every night before bed using a special threader to go under and over my bridge and between my teeth. I use a rubber tip to massage my gums and remove more plaque. This is followed by cleaning my tongue with a scraper and using a dry toothbrush inside my front lower teeth, where we all gather more saliva and plaque when we eat and drink.

Lastly, I apply a prescription fluoride toothpaste to my teeth that is not rinsed, another preventative practice to maintain healthy teeth and gums. My nightly habit takes about ten minutes. I can't go to sleep without performing this practice. It has become an important, habitual part of my life, no different from taking my daily shower.

In addition, I must take care not to bite into any hard food such as an apple or corn on the cob. I am always cautious and eat certain foods with my side teeth or avoid them altogether. The fork and knife are my helpers. My oral practices are an essential health regime in my life.

As I have grown and healed throughout the years, my appearance has always been important. I strived to be my healthy best. I see myself as elegant and attractive, with imperfect beauty. I am a well-groomed, neatly dressed woman who takes pride in her appearance and in her achievements.

CHAPTER 26:
SELF-ACTUALIZATION
AND PROCLAMATION

In 2017, Ricky and I decided to pursue our next venture: we were aging and seeking a new home for our retirement. So, after much searching, we moved into a cozy house in Windsor, California. Being in the forty-fifth year of my nursing career, I decided to scale my work time back to three days a week. I took a position with Sonoma County Behavioral Health, working in their mental health urgent care department, diagnosing mental illnesses and prescribing needed medications. I took medical histories and performed physical exams on individuals in the crisis stabilization unit, pending inpatient admission. I also performed some medical primary care, managing illnesses such as urinary tract infections, elevated blood sugars, minor injuries, and pain. I referred patients to the emergency department when necessary.

The following year I went down to working two days a week, continuing to work at Sonoma County Mental Health Outpatient Services, I stayed until May 2019. My goal was to reduce my work hours and pursue other hobbies such as dance, music, yoga, cooking, reading, fitness, and writing my memoirs. Ricky and I loved being close to the ocean, the beach, and traveling to the redwoods and the rolling, regional Coastal Cascades. We have learned to be wine snobs and great food snobs, but still kind people, and we enjoyed the many friends and acquaintances we have made along the way.

In October, 2018 we met our newest granddaughter, Sophie, our seventh grandchild. We made a decision to return to Kansas City in order to be closer to the children, their spouses and the other six grandchildren, Ben; Noel; Adam; Jonah; Julia and Oliver. So, in March of 2019 we traveled to Kansas City to buy a new home. We found one and sold our home in northern California. We look forward to continuing our life's journey together, embarking, yet again, on a new chapter of our anecdote. In addition, we have gained a Boston Terrier dog—Zoe. She brings joy to our lives.

I may continue to work part-time here and there, as I enjoy caring for people with special needs, connecting with my feelings of love, fear, and grace remain ongoing as I remember my past experiences. They give me strength and compassion for others, as well as perseverance to continue working on inner harmony.

Therefore, I proclaim that being a woman with facial difference has not been a deterrent to being a functioning, productive, happy individual in the world. Every day my personal growth continues as

I pursue my interests and goals—and my ongoing oral health. I realize that I dwell in possibility and that anything that is imaginable is achievable. My goal is to be healthy and joyful! My imperfect beauty has been an asset for me. I embrace being different. Perfect!

As mentioned in the beginning, I want my story to convey to others with facial difference that you, too, are capable of doing anything you want to do. Grasp your gift of life. The universe does take care of us. We all have a story to tell. I am delighted to have had the opportunity to share mine lovingly, to inspire others.

I would like to end my tale with one of my most poignant poems:

"Pretty Lady"

I am a pretty lady.

I know that it is true.

My smile is very bright,

Shining through and through.

I am a pretty lady.

I feel so warm inside.

My eyes glow with happiness.

It feels so right.

I am a pretty lady.

I've got so much class.

As I walk so tall.

You may stare as I pass.

I am a pretty lady.

With a style of my own.

I know that I am different.

A rhythm with unique tone.

I am a pretty lady.

You need not tell me so.

I've got a special look that only belongs to me.

And feeling oh so pretty, has set me free.

Free to feel good about myself.

Free to live in peace without a doubt.

BIBLIOGRAPHY

Bhattacharya, S, V Khanna, and R Kohli, "Cleft Lip: The Historical Perspective," *Indian Journal of Plastic Surgery,* no. 42(S01) (October 2009): S4-S8.

   https://www.ncbi.nim.nih.gov/pmc/articles/PMC2825059/.

Center for Disease Control, "Facts about Cleft Lip and Cleft Palate," (December 05, 2019): 1-3. httpwww.cdc.gov/ncbddd/birthde-fects/cleftlip.html.

Drabkin, Alan. "Stat Consult: Cleft Lip and Palate," *The Clinical Advisor,* (August 03, 2018): 15. https://www.clinicaladvisor. com stat-consult-cleft-lip-and-palate/printarticle/786001/.

Gallagher, Grace; medically reviewed by Cobb, Cynthia, DNP, APRN, "Everything to Know about Your Cupid's Bow," *Healthline.* (June 22, 2020):1-7. https://

www.healthline.com/health/beauty-skin-care/
everthing-to-know-about-your-cupids- bow#takeaway.

March of Dimes, "Who We Are," (2019):1-2. https://marchofdimes.
org/mission/who-we-are.aspx.

McManus, David E." Reiki is Better Than Placebo and Has Broad
Potential as a Complementary Health Therapy," *Journal of
Evidence Based Complementary Alternative Medicine,* no.4
(October 22, 2017): 1051-1057. https://ncbi.nim.nih.gov/pmc/
articles/PMC5871310/.

Patel, Pravin K, Stephanie Cohen, Raja Ramaswamy, Mitchell F
Grasseschi, Mary O'Gara, Erin K McGraw, Francisco Talavera,
S Anthony Wolfe, Jorge I de la Torre, chief ed. "Cleft Palate
Repair," *Medscape/emedicine.,* (June 14, 2018 and updated
on June, 05, 2020):1-9. htpps://emedicine.medscape.com/
article/1279283-overview.

Rand, William, Reiki, *The Healing touch, First and Second
Degree Manual: Including Japanese Reiki Techniques and
Hayashi Healing Guide Additions.* Southfield, MI: Vision
Publications, 2000.

Shirol S.S., "Sociocultural Beliefs and Perceptions about Cleft Lip-
Palate and Their Implications in the Management, Outcome
and Rehabilitation," *Journal of Cleft Lip Palate and Craniofacial
Anomalies,* 5, no.1 (February 08, 2018):4-5. https://www.
clpca.org/article.asp?issn=2348-2125;year=2018:volume=5;is-
sue=1;spage=4;epage=5;aulast=Shirol-abstract.

Smile Train, "Every Child Deserves the Ability to Smile; We Want Our Cause to be Yours," (2019), 1-6. https://www.smiletrain.org/our-cause.

Wide Smiles, "Harelip"-The Dark Side of an Unfortunate Word," (1996):1-2. https://www.widesmiles.org/cleftlinks/WS-159, html.

Winston, Robert and Rebecca Chicot, "The Importance of Early Bonding on the Long-Term Mental Health and Resilience of Children," London *Journal of Primary Care*, (February 24, 2016) 8(1):12-14. http://creativecommons.org/licenses/by/4.0/.